D1613018

ENTREPRENEUR SUCCESS FORMULA

HOW THRIVING BUSINESS OWNERS ACTUALLY DO IT

By **Damian Mark Smyth**

(The Entrepreneurs Circle's Mindset Coach)

"A great read and a person worth following, he will help you master yourself" - Dave Stickland, Retail Expert, CEO & Founder at Store Guru Ltd

"The principles, ideas and case studies in this book are inspiring" - AJB

"Every entrepreneur who realises the importance of working on their own thinking to become successful will value this book" - Cheryl Salmon, The French Translation Company

"This is an excellent book for helping you to get the correct mindset for establishing a really successful business. Highly recommended" - Amazon Reader

"Plenty of practical information which can easily be implemented, leading to great results!" - Emre Gurler, Office Hut Ltd

"What a great read this is. One of those where your partner asks you to 'Put the iPad down and go to sleep!'" - Mat Butler, Director at Business Video Experts

"I read a lot of books and often they give you the topline details of 'success' but not the practical tips and help and the 'how'. As well as encouraging you to start with your own 'why' (why are you in business, what difference will you make?), this book gives you how other people have done it - in enough detail that you can actually do the stuff in it" - Amazon Reader

"If you want to get on and need help to see the bones of what you need to do to succeed, then 'The Entrepreneur Success Formula' is a book with implementable strategies, practical advice... all supported with real life examples and should be at the top of your reading list" - Paul Field, Owner of WFP Fire & Security

"There are many great books that business owners can study in order to improve their chances of success. This book goes a step further by clearly explaining options to overcoming the main barriers. It's one for the bookshelf that you'll want to keep referring back to" - Jan Long, Southampton Tuition Centre

"A great read for anyone whether just starting a business or been in business for years" - David Logan

3

Damian Mark Smyth is the author of: *How to be Stress Free in 24 Hours*, *Anger Gone* and *Do Nothing!* and is the Mindset Coach for the Entrepreneurs Circle. He lives in Berkshire with his partner, Victoria, their two children Annie-Rose and Micah and Wellington the greedy Labrador

For all of my Family, but especially Alannah, Aoife, Annie-Rose and Micah

THE ELEMENTS:

PREFACE

"If your 'secret' is so great, where's my Ferrari...?!"

I have a question for you. Why don't self-help books work for the majority of their readers? The answer is actually quite simple. The 'method', which worked for the writer of the book, works for them... so they expect it will work for everyone else as well. But of course, everyone is different, which is why this book you are reading is also very different from other books because it contains a formula for success accumulated from thousands upon thousands of successful business owners... and not just one. It's actually a book about the system 'behind' success. What makes it all work in the first place... for everyone.

You see, there are systems and processes in everything we do. The very act of you reading this book involves a series of intricate systems to make it happen successfully. But everyone will be reading this sentence ever so slightly differently to everyone else, despite using the same system (words/

eyesight). You'll all be in a different location with different lighting. You will all have different histories and expectations and different thoughts currently in your heads. But the system to make the reading itself successful is sound and explainable and is a superb method to get the ideas across... how you apply the acquired knowledge you gain from the system used, is entirely down to you.

This book is therefore not just an opinion. It's a distillation of years of experience in helping entrepreneurs become more successful in their own businesses and an understanding about how the system which delivers success works. It's a formula which has been accumulated by looking at systems and processes and by applying the stand out successful behaviours and actions to a multitude of different businesses in a multitude of different industries and sectors and seeing the results time and time again.

The business owners who've been a part of this process, who've found out what does and doesn't work, are the guinea pigs in this particular laboratory. You get to reap the benefit of the lessons they've already learned on your behalf. From one man band start-ups to multi-million pound franchises, the Entrepreneurs Circle (correct, no apostrophe) has helped them all, with every aspect of business from getting the right staff, to marketing to the right customers, from creating audacious goals, to actually achieving them by having the right mindset and of course, implementing and testing the results. As a business coach with decades of experience in helping business owners achieve success, and as the Mindset Coach within the Entrepreneurs Circle, I will be the 'scientist' delivering the data in the form of a research paper (in this case called 'a book') with real life case studies to back it up as evidence. As the entrepreneur, or would-be entrepreneur, it is up to you to apply the success formula to your own business (or idea for one), and see the results for yourself.

Damian Mark Smyth,

January 2016

INTRODUCTION

"If we did all the things we are capable of, we would literally astound ourselves." - Thomas A. Edison

From this precise moment onwards, your life can be very different. But only if you choose it to be. You see, everything you have in your life around you right now, all the possessions you own, the relationships you have, the career and life purpose which you are fulfilling, and the success or otherwise of all of these ventures, is a result of one thing and one thing only... the choices you have made up until now. No one else has had this power over your destiny, only you. Even when events have been out of your hands, such as being involved in a car crash caused by someone else, the way you react to this event is still a choice and is therefore still your own.

Choice is the gift we have all been given to navigate our own vessels (body and mind) through the sea of life. It's a powerful and devious little tool all at the same time, but it's yours, and you need to fully realise and understand that if you don't make the choices in your life, someone else will make them for you.

This book is all about how you make those choices and how you can apply them day in and day out. It's a formula for success, which thousands of entrepreneurs have followed and you can choose to follow too. But it's also a book about character, because who you become as you succeed, is just as, if not more important than what you have to do to get there. You'll need to think very hard about why you chose to become an Entrepreneur - at least that is why I am assuming you're reading a book with a title such as this.

Why did you choose to become someone who takes extraordinary risks, and disregard the safety of a full-time permanent position, with all its camaraderie, perks and fun, for the incessant 4.00am hikes into a mental torture wilderness of anxiety and stress over lost shipments, 20+ hour days, stagnated cash flow, under-performing staff and untrustworthy suppliers?

If you've already taken the entrepreneurial plunge, I bet you ask yourself this question frequently. If you're about to make the leap into the unknown, you may be unaware of this torment, but then you're also probably hoping this book will help you solve at least some, or even most of these issues. Either way, you'll be looking for a process to make your business successful and I have some really good news for you - this book will do more than just that. It'll give you a tried and tested, step by step formula to apply to your business, along with essential elements to ensure business success. But it will also tell you a great deal... about you - who you need to become to achieve the steps laid out on the following pages.

A 'formula' according to the Dictionary, is "A set form of words used for stating or declaring something definitely or authoritatively, for indicating the procedure to be followed, or is any fixed or conventional method for doing something." Not that what you are about to read is 'conventional' by any means, as you'll soon see.

Bearing in mind that, according to Bloomberg, 8 out of 10 entrepreneurs who start businesses fail within the first 18 months - that's a whopping 80% who will crash and burn - it takes a certain type of person, one with guts and determination to want to become an entrepreneur. So for the sake of the next few hours in my company, I'll assume that the reason you picked up this book is because you're one of those wonderful individuals who sees opportunity, rather than problems in life. Someone who looks at events through rather different lenses, those of... 'positive change' - because if you're in business, you're in the business of change and unless you're a wheel clamper (apologies if you actually are a wheel clamper - I'm sure educating the general public on parking restrictions through extortion has its uses) then you are in the business of change for the positive and that is why you have a business at all or are thinking of starting one.

Unless you make a positive change in someone else's life, there is no 'value exchange' and if there is no value exchange, there is no business. You find someone else's problem and you make it go away. It really is that simple. Of course, you'll require customers who pay you something to have this solution, but bear in mind that the value of this solution and the positive change it brings is down to the 'positioning' of your product or service and the 'perception' of your clients. This book will formulate how to execute both of these in a way that will make entrepreneurial success easier to come by.

Although there are many great books on entrepreneurship and many 'must-reads' for the wannabe entrepreneur, such as The E-Myth Revisited by Michael Gerber (see the links at back of the book), there is no clear formula for entrepreneurial success laid out step-by-step for the reader to follow and specifically one that has the 'being' part as well as the 'doing' part - because who you are is just as, if not more, important than what you do. Mainly because one drives the other, but also because you will encounter difficulties along the way (yes, even with a formula) and who you are will determine your reaction to these bumps in the road. In fact, it will be the most crucial element that decides whether you are in the 20% who succeed or the 80% who crash and burn.

How do I know this? Well, as a coach, author and keynote speaker, I coach entrepreneurs. Just entrepreneurs, no one else. I write about entrepreneurship - nothing else. And I speak daily to entrepreneurs (and pretty much no one else apart from the postman and occasional supermarket cashier) about entrepreneurship. I used to coach other folk before, but entrepreneurs are far more challenging and way more fun and you are all doing it for the same reason whether you know it or not, and I'm here to help you make positive changes for more of your customers by helping you to make your business really successful.

Through years of helping thousands of business owners just like you to grow and succeed and in my current role as Senior Business Growth Expert for the UK's largest entrepreneur support network - I ultimately help entrepreneurs become more effective at positive change through addressing the way they think. Over the years, I've noticed many similar behaviours, attitudes and values in my clients. Some useful and some less so. Yes, other people see problems... but you, with your special 'opportunity X-Ray vision', see a chance for a change for the better. However, until you can successfully effect that change and make it into a sustainable and profitable business model, it is about as useful as a handbrake on a canoe. Although I'm aware that the reason some of you went into business was because "If you want something doing, you might as well do it yourself," but if that means 20+ hour days and your children forgetting your name, then it's not working very well!

What if you could reclaim your entrepreneurial mojo and remember why it was you started this epic journey into madness? What if you could snuggle up in the cozy warmth of the following pages, safe in the knowledge that within, lies the required information to show you how to get back on track and become part of that tiny percentage of businesses who actually make a go of it, succeed and even thrive, first or second time around? How would that feel?

You see, on a daily basis as part of my role at the Entrepreneurs Circle, I get to work with all sorts of entrepreneurial businesses, from start-ups to multi-million pound franchises. We have literally thousands of successful clients and are cultivating more daily and it's why I've chosen to take the knowledge I've gained from working with these businesses and business owners over the years and decided to make the lessons available to a wider audience. Most specifically, it's the thinking behind the success that separates the really high achievers from the rest and all of the case studies in this book have been written by successful members of the Entrepreneurs Circle, who think differently and do differently as a result.

The systems and processes you will be hearing about in this book have worked for thousands of successful businesses, but don't get fooled by thinking it's all about the systems. It's not. It's not even about the formula. It's about one system and one system only.

When you understand this system which underpins everything else, you will see that who you have to become to succeed whilst implementing the formula, is what will make it work. Which is why this particular book has been written specifically to change you, from the inside out. Who you become as a result of following the steps outlined within these pages will ensure your future success.

I should know, as I've had more than my own fair share of challenges along the way to my own, but you'll hear snippets of my story, (especially the bit about emerging from someone with Obsessive Compulsive Disorder, OCD - to speaking on stage in front of 1,200 people, sharing stages with Apple Co-founder Steve Wozniak and Michael E. Gerber) as we go through the book. For now though, let's go right back to the beginning and start with probably the most important question you need to answer for yourself to make your business succeed: Why did you do it?

Now if you're looking for a magic bullet to make your business thrive, I've got some bad news for you. It'll take a great deal of hard work and some wrong turns along the way and unless you have a very good reason for taking this leap into the unknown, then

you'll probably give up before you get the chance
to learn how to even survive, let alone thrive. Why
is there such a demand for the 'quick-win'? Well,
we live in a world where we expect fast results. The
reason so many online marketers do so well with their
info-products is because they play to an audience who
demands a quick-fix - an immediate 'one-stop-shop'
to solve their problems. We'd all love to think there's
an easy way to do it. We look at other businesses and
wonder how they manage to make it all look so simple
and effortless. But that's the problem. They didn't find
it easy at all, it just looks as if they did.

I've never met anyone who's had an easy-ride to
success, not even multi-millionaires who've been
cash positive since day one. Money (in particular cash
flow) is definitely part of the problem and the solution.
However, it's by no means the only player in the game.
I've heard too many stories of well-funded individuals
who've still managed to screw their business up, to
prove my point.

There are a number of elements within the formula,
which need to be applied to make a business succeed
and there is never a quick-fix or a simple solution.
However, if you have the right mindset and enough of

these elements in place and consistently apply them in the right order, success will surely follow.

Just because we see businesses who are succeeding, doesn't mean they found these elements first time around and implemented them straight away. Theirs was also a long hard journey into long, hard nights to make the discoveries required to find the ones which worked, to then implement them on more long, hard days, to then test and recalibrate before success was even a glimpse on the distant horizon. It was the persistence that kept them going, not a magic formula. So don't ever judge a book by its cover when it comes to coveting another's seemingly easy ride. What you see is not the reality behind the story.

Just look at the recent Hollywood blockbuster 'The Imitation Game', where Alan Turing was depicted as the outcast homosexual genius who altered the course of the Second World War after overhearing a story in a bar about a German spy. It certainly didn't happen in the way depicted. Bill Tutte was the man whose discovery changed the course of the War, and it happened when he was alone, not in a bar. What's more, the machine code Bill deciphered was the more advanced Lorenz, not the Enigma device. Alan Turing did not even break the code of Enigma as the film suggests, a Polish scientist called Marian Rejewski can lay claim to that. But even the way this profound insight occurred whilst out on the town was inaccurate. Turing contributed to the breaking of the Enigma code through sheer grit and determination and solid hard work. But then a story of hard work and continuous slog doesn't sell popcorn. Artistic license, most definitely. Truth, no.

Conversely, the advice and stories laid out within these pages are more akin to the reality of the story of the teams of code breakers at Bletchley Park. They have been aggregated from years of support to business owners through my own coaching and now working with the Entrepreneurs Circle, with their own stories of success and failure (a much-maligned word and crucial part of the process by the way), and the subsequent learnings gained, which have nurtured and grown successful businesses as a result. These are the real systems, processes and truths that will catapult you to your own entrepreneurial success. After all, why reinvent the wheel when you can benefit from other people's mistakes and subsequent lessons learned?

There is, however, one element that made both

the code breaking of Enigma and Lorenz possible: Applied mathematics. It was a constant, underlying the success in solving a supposedly unsolvable puzzle. In this regard, there is also one crucial element that I would ask you to decipher as you read the pages in this book. I call it the 'Entrepreneurial Base Element' and although it's the mainstay of most successful endeavours, it's also hardly ever discussed. But every successful entrepreneur and new venture business that I have ever met, has it. Funnily enough, it's not what you may be thinking. It's not your 'why', which we'll address next. But see if you can spot it in the coming pages as you delve into the elements of the Entrepreneur Success Formula and begin your own journey to entrepreneurial success.

21

Entrepreneur Success Formula

ELEMENT ONE: START WITH WHY: YOUR BUSINESS ROCKET FUEL

"He who has a strong enough why, can bear almost any how" - Friedrich Nietzsche

Launching a business is actually very simple. Anyone can come up with a name, start a limited company and create a brand. Just go to ClickBank.com or JVZoo.com, set up an account and pick a white label product to resell. Then go to LeadPages.net and set up a holding page and PeoplePerHour.co.uk or Upwork or Fiverr.com to find a designer to create a logo design. Create a payment account on PayPal. com, rustle up a 'Buy Now' button, add some code to your squeeze page on Leadpages.net, sign up for some list capture activity with MailChimp, bung in some autoresponders, and that's about it really.

You have a product to sell and somewhere to sell it and a process to capture and nurture leads. Of course, you now need to find customers to buy your product, but even that bit's easy - there's a chapter that deals with that later on. So on the basis that 'this business lark' is a complete doddle, why isn't everyone smashing it all the way to a beach in the Bahamas?

Life, and especially business, is never that simple. For a start, some businesses begin their entrepreneurial journey with the wrong product, but most start with entirely the wrong business model. They start with the premise that people buy predominantly on price. Some do. Some don't, and for the sake and ease of your own journey, unless you're absolutely rolling in spare cash, I suggest you think about the latter type of customer first. If you're contemplating the price conscious option and someone else wants to copy your business model and nab your customers, they'll only have to offer your product or service at a lower price and you lose your customer and your sale as a result. What's more, your competitor loses profitability and you're both in a downward spiral of cost cutting and margin slashing, which is simply not sustainable.

Then there's the biggest problem of all... You. Yes, you'll start with a spring in your step for sure, but that spring will soon turn to a lull and then a lollop as you begin to procrastinate on the simplest tasks and get sidetracked by other ventures with your cash flow and enthusiasm dwindling. In fact, the biggest problem I see when I speak to my clients is staring me in the face, literally.

I mentioned previously that who you are is more important than what you'll be doing. And in that regard, your 'why' is the element that will get you through the hard times and push you to do what is necessary to succeed and thrive. You see, there is only one reason why anyone is in business in the first place... as I already mentioned in the introduction, your product or service makes a positive change in someone else's life. To whatever degree you make a positive difference in your customers' lives and how much that change is worth to them, will determine the success or otherwise of your business.

Now 'value' and 'worth' are very different from 'price'. Think about some of the brands you trust personally. Why do you trust them? What is it about that brand that makes you come back time and again for more and know they will deliver? Is it the price? I doubt it. In fact, we tend to trust the brands that cost us more, not less.

We talk a great deal in the Entrepreneurs Circle about Simon Sinek, an author and speaker whose books and programmes delve into what inspires customers to buy. His TEDx talk can be found here: bit.ly/TEDxSimonSinek. In this short presentation he shows that 'People don't buy what you do, they buy why you do it', using Apple as an example. Effectively, we are more likely to buy from people we know, like and trust who have the same values and beliefs as us. Therefore, it's important that we know what those values are and make sure others are able to identify with them.

There will no doubt be a very good reason 'why' you do what you do, or are about to do. It may well be that you decided to start your business because you care passionately about the positive change you wish to make for others. You may have seen an opportunity to make a real difference in the world, whilst at the same time creating a viable business, which could give value to your family and community. You may have seen others provide the same product or service and decided you could deliver it better. Or you might just be doing it for a change of scenery, or maybe even because you have to do it. Whatever reason you have for taking the plunge, you'll definitely want to be making enough money to make it worthwhile.

I want to make something clear first though, 'to get rich' is not a reason why you do what you do - even if you think it is. Receiving monetary reward is a result of what you do, not a reason for doing it. You might want to have financial freedom and security for yourself and your family, (that's a pretty good 'why') but just saying you want to be rich, is not enough. I've seen too many unhappy millionaires to realise that money is not the key to happiness, it's simply a tool to assist us to do the 'stuff' we love - and in the case of those with a terminal illness and a bulging bank balance - sometimes it's not even very good at that.

"I wanted my kids to know me, I wasn't always there for them, and I wanted them to know why and to understand what I did." - Steve Jobs on his deathbed

No one actually really wants to 'be rich' - even the flash cars and bling and rolling around in wads of cash, which we see all over music videos, is actually pointing to a much deeper desire. The freedom which an abundance of money could bring... the precious time spent with a loved one... the tiny momentary fragments where time stands still and life just rocks...

the imagined perfect sunset... the touch from someone who connects with our soul... our own child's loving smile... we can even imagine it as if it were a reality that lasts forever, believing that money could somehow buy it... but you're looking in the wrong direction for that particular treasure. Your imaginations are possible and money may well be required to facilitate some of them - but there is a more important driving force beyond this 'standard of deferred payment' that needs to be recognised first.

Richard Bach, author of 'Jonathan Livingston Seagull' said: "Here is the test to find whether your mission on Earth is finished: if you're alive, it isn't." I'm assuming, as you are reading this that you're alive, so you have a purpose and are hopefully willing to find out what it might be...? [My recent TED talk goes into discovering your purpose on a deeper level: bit.ly/damiantedtalk].

Is there something keeping you awake at night? I'm not talking about the next-door neighbours arguing over the school run, or the alley-cat singing late into the night. I'm talking about that little voice inside your head that's been trying to tell you something. It's the same one that drove you to read this book and the same one that's been telling you 'you're onto something', when you first had the idea to set up in business. It's the voice of insight that tells you where your car keys actually are, just as you make the seventeenth attempt to find them in their regular place!

But whether you are already in business or not, the Apple founder Steve Jobs referred to your purpose as 'Making your dent on the Universe'. The fact is, everything that has ever happened in the history of the entire Universe up until this very point in existence, has led to you reading these words, right now... What are you here on earth to do? Are you going to leave this mortal coil a slightly better place than it was when you were born? And if so, what are you planning to do to make a positive difference in the world? The value will not be in the sales you make... the value will be in the difference you make.

Your 'reason' therefore, for taking a leap into the unknown will need to be strong enough to survive some pretty jarring bumps in the road. The times when you wondered why on earth you started this journey in the first place. The times when you take a sideways glance at the jobs section in the paper, just to see 'what's out there'. The times when your cash flow doesn't quite cover the wages and you wonder what the hell you're going to do to stop a full-blown riot. The times you might not have experienced yet and hopefully, with the help of this book, you won't have to - but there are plenty of other tricky situations that might well happen in the coming months and years ahead - and it's your 'why' (and your wisdom) that will pull you through them. The end result may well be those imagined dreams and a life of freedom, but by then you'll be someone entirely different. You'll have become who you need to be in order to achieve your dreams. And that, is far more powerful than the dreams themselves...

Whatever your reason for deciding to take the entrepreneurial plunge, I would like you to start to think about why you do what you do by answering the following questions. Take a few moments somewhere quiet and think about them before writing down your answers:

- Why does (or will) your business exist - what is its purpose?
- Why do you and your staff get out of bed in the morning (and it can't be 'for the money')?

- Why would your market and the world be a poorer place if your business simply ceased to exist?

- What do you generate beyond profit and what impact do your activities have on your people, your communities and the larger world?

- What is your own mission or purpose?

The questions above are meant to get your thought processes started in the right direction, because what I've seen over the years is that the business owners who do really well, have a lot more right thinking than the ones who don't. What do I mean by 'right thinking'? As I mentioned earlier, everything you see in your life around you right now - all the possessions you own, the career you've carved out for yourself, the relationships you have - are the results of the choices you've made up until now. And all of those choices were as a result of the thinking you had prior to making that choice. If you didn't have the thought "I'll set up a business...," you wouldn't have made the choice to become an entrepreneur. Same applies for your relationships and all the things you possess. Prior to deciding to either commit to buy or commit to commit, you made a choice, which involved thinking first.

As we go deeper into the book, you'll start to see a pattern emerging. 'Right thinking' is really just another way of saying 'clarity' or 'insight', and when you have clarity on anything, it's easier to make a decision about it... and when it's easy to make a decision on something, that's when you take decisive and effective action. What I've noticed time and time again over the years is that the entrepreneurs who take clear, decisive action are the ones who succeed. The ones who overthink things are the ones who stagnate, stall and ultimately fail.

The longest journey starts with a single step and the best thing you can do to succeed, is to start. I've run numerous training courses for entrepreneurs at the Entrepreneurs Circle's National Support Centre in Birmingham, including one particular course on book writing, and the number of wannabe authors who've come to the day and promised to do the actions necessary - 500 words a day for three months - but still fail... is staggering! With the best intentions, they promised to deliver, but couldn't do it. And the reason is simple. They got stuck in their thinking. They over-thought the book, so they ended up writing half a book instead, or they procrastinated and ended up writing no book at all, along with the trillions of other brilliant, yet unsuccessful and unwritten books throughout history (some of which would have been best-sellers!). Once you have a clear idea of why you do what you do and where you want to go with it, it's like someone putting rocket fuel into your tank. You've decided to make the journey. You know why you want to make it and you're feeling inspired to take that first step, and your 'why' is going to get you off the launch pad. It's going to give you the necessary thrust and momentum to get past the initial stages, beyond the atmosphere and into orbit.

But here's the real kicker: your 'why', can change! That's correct, your 'why' can develop as your success grows. Your initial reason for starting the business will always remain the same, but why you continue and why you decide to grow can and probably will, change. This is, therefore, more akin to the direction your business is headed, which is why the next element is so crucial in the Entrepreneur Success Formula. You'll need clarity on your destination before you start the journey, but not for the reasons you may be thinking.

I once heard that if a Jumbo-Jet is sitting on the tarmac at London Heathrow and the nose of the aircraft is just one millimeter out from its intended target of JFK airport in New York, it would land hundreds of miles away (if it flew in a straight line). Likewise, if your destination is unclear, then you may land somewhere different to your intended target. The Jumbo-Jet happens to have a self-correcting mechanism on board and in many ways, that's how entrepreneurs should think of 'insight', something to recalibrate them when they fly off-course.

So often I've started to work with entrepreneurs who feel 'lost', and when I ask them where they're going and where they are right now, they can't tell me. "It's no wonder you feel lost then isn't it?!" Like ships bobbing around on the ocean with nowhere to go and no idea where they came from... yes, you might feel a little lost!

The degree of clarity you have at start-up will not therefore necessarily define your destination so much as it defines your thinking and the subsequent choices and habits you adopt in the weeks and months ahead. And this is where it gets really interesting, because so many businesses focus too heavily on the goal as the most important element, but how many times have you met people who've actually achieved exactly what they set out to achieve in the first place? Rarely? Never...?! Of course, you'll need to adjust as you go along, why wouldn't you? Unexpected events will always knock you off balance. That's called life. Of course, you'll be willing to recalibrate and get yourself back on track and if your 'why' is strong enough to start with, it will always set you back on the right path, which is why goal setting per se, is at the same time crucial and also a complete waste of time. The clarity you get whilst doing it, is the most important element in the formula here.

So now's the time to get some of that clarity on your destination, as we delve into the next chapter on 'Goal Setting'.

CASE STUDY: GRAHAM HILL AT VERBATIM

Verbatim, The Telephone Answering Service, was launched on 15th April 1997, but Graham's journey as an entrepreneur started on August 2nd, 1990 when Sadam Hussain invaded Kuwait. This event prevented his first attempt at owning a successful business, but seven years later he launched his fourth business after two more failures and one 'reasonable' success. Why did Graham continue his journey in becoming an entrepreneur?

"Apart from three children and my lovely wife Juliet to support, there are four reasons that were and still are my driving force. I didn't want to return to corporate life and be a wage slave with all the politics which that entailed. I wanted to develop a business model with recurring revenue - the venture before Verbatim comprised publishing over twenty local advertising directories in the Thames Valley - and if I didn't sell space every week, I couldn't afford to put food on the table. I also wanted to create a business that could make a real difference to our clients and one my staff would be proud to represent. And finally, I wanted a business that would hold my passion by delivering outstanding customer service and real returns for my clients for many years, and I am as excited and passionate about what we do now as I was back in 1997.

For any budding entrepreneur starting out or needing a change in direction, my advice would be to never, ever give up, because the harder you try, the luckier you will get and it's all too easy to fall at the first hurdle and not recover.

Aside from the earlier failures, we frequently hit the buffers in the first stages of Verbatim too. Our initial business plans revolved around pre-selling 40 contracts to an existing client base of 600-800 regular advertising customers, most of whom were quality local trade businesses serving the property market. This meant we should have revenue of around £1,500 per month in place to pay the wages for our first receptionist and to rent a tiny office. We agreed a contract with British Telecom to install 40 ISDN and Dial Direct Lines on January 1st 1997 and to save some cash, I was going to do the book-keeping and VAT returns myself.

But we didn't sell 40 contracts, or even 30 and not even anywhere near 20. We only sold a paltry 4 contracts and there I was thinking I was a great salesman! I simply hadn't factored in the negative attitude of sole-traders working for immediate wages, versus those who were expanding their businesses and looking at call answering as a potential solution. They simply didn't grasp the concept that the Entrepreneurs Circle screams about today... "Answer the b****y phones, because if you don't, your competitors will and you'll lose the business!"

With just a few days until the launch of January 1st and with only four clients to pay us, BT were late installing our lines. We didn't end up going live until April 15th, some 100 days later than planned. Picture this - no market - no income, start-up loans for capital equipment installed at £150,000 - rent and wages to pay, without any essential infrastructure to service our customers - and not even many of them, for that matter. Can you imagine what would have happened to our reputation if I had managed to pre-sell those other 36 contracts? Which is where we had a double dose of Lady Luck.

In those days, BT paid out £25 per day, per line, in compensation for late installation. We ended up receiving a cheque in May for £18,000. This kept us afloat and gave us some time whilst we changed our strategy (BT have since changed their T&C's as a result of our claim). Not one to give up and with my overriding passionate belief that the business would actually work, we tried a new tack by writing to over 40 business we knew in the professional services sector - accountants, solicitors and management training consultants. Our objective this time was not to sell to them but to ask for help to introduce us to business owners who they knew and might benefit from our services. We got a bite from a London-based franchisee of a Canadian training company saying that this was just what they were looking for. Nearly 20 years later and we still service them as a client.

The unplanned delay gave us the time to change direction from our original target market to the professional service sector, who were more attuned to the concept of a personal reception service, delivering an enhanced experience to their customers. They also understood that one missed call could result in lost sales and profits.

Twenty years later, and after answering over five million calls and delivering well over one million new sales inquiries to small business owners and entrepreneurs, we are about to launch a new global telephone answering software product. None of this would have happened if we had fallen at the first hurdle and given up. My 'why' has kept me going and my passion has never wavered to deliver outstanding customer service whilst improving my clients bottom line."

www.verbatim-cc.co.uk

ELEMENT TWO: GOAL SETTING: WHY CLARITY THROUGH PLANNING REALLY MATTERS, BUT PLANS HARDLY MATTER AT ALL!

"What stands in the way, becomes the way"
- Marcus Aurelius

What is a goal? A goal is something to aim for. It gives you a purpose or a sense of direction toward which you can point your energies and efforts. Goals are also the targets toward which you point your daily habits, whether in small, simple ways, like knowing you need food and thinking how to get it by imagining yourself jumping in the car and driving to the shops, or more audacious goals such as writing a best-selling book, getting married or starting a new business.

Whatever size and time scale you have in mind, goal setting is a very useful and powerful tool, but not for the reasons you may have been told. Its real strengths lie in being able to assist you in accomplishing your life's visions and creating good habits. As I've already suggested, it's the clarity you get whilst planning and the subsequent habits and behaviours you adopt as a result of goal setting that really matters here. Who you become by achieving your goal is way more important than the goal will ever be. In this chapter, you'll learn how to use goals to do just that.

Firstly though, I want to ask you to picture something in your mind: imagine an architect, a structural engineer and a builder discussing the construction of your dream home on a large plot of land, a house you've designed personally. The builder thinks he knows what you want from what he thought he heard from the structural engineer, but the architect isn't sure and there's an argument ensuing. You'd probably be quite concerned if this scenario was playing out in reality. And rightly so!

Trying to build a house without a blueprint would be crazy, especially if you weren't doing all of the work yourself, (but even then it would be hard). How would your ideas come across using only the spoken word and Chinese whispers? Yes, it's still possible without a plan, but it's so much easier with one. But something even more important happens when ideas are put into writing. Clarity emerges. Having ideas written down in a language that everyone can speak is one thing, but putting them on paper in your own language brings up challenges and issues which may not have crossed your mind, until they were staring you in the face on paper.

Imagine also that there were no fixed time limits for the build. Calendars hadn't been invented yet and there was no way of synchronising all of the parts of the project. No one knows who will be doing what and by when. Total chaos! Which is why writing things down on a calendar or in a diary also brings clarity. You see, humans have an incredible talent to be able to transport themselves into a future which isn't happening, or hasn't happened yet. They can envisage something that doesn't exist and make plans to make it into reality, or see it as real in the present moment.

I asked you to do that just now by imagining your house build. You were able to imagine a builder, an architect, a structural engineer and a plot of land... perhaps even a dream home and an argument as well! Now it's absolutely impossible that you will have had the same thoughts as anyone else reading this book, so this is where written goals and clarity come in handy (everyone sees life differently - which is an important aspect we will discuss later on).

Look at everything around you now. Everything you see started off as a thought in someone's mind first. And to make that thought into the tables, chairs, cars, seats, or wherever you happen to be and whatever is there, these ideas had to be written down first and clarified. It had to be imagined to be achieved first, and then it had to be clarified to be made real.

The same applies in your business. It needs to be imagined first and then put into writing to get the clarity you require to start making it into a reality. The extent to which you envisage the future and get clear on your goals will then determine the habits that you maintain to make this happen. We'll be discussing habits in more detail a bit later on.

Without a clear plan and clear goals, you can end up going around and around in circles living an unproductive and hectic life (sound familiar?). This is usually the first point of call when dealing with someone who procrastinates. I use the example in training courses, that if your mobile phone buzzed an emergency tone and it was from a loved one who'd been rushed to hospital, would you procrastinate before you got up and left? Clear goals (get to hospital) clear plan (get in car and drive - fast).

We spend so much time doing unproductive 'stuff' simply because there isn't enough clarity on why we're doing anything in the first place. There are other reasons that we procrastinate of course, such as fear of failure or even success, but these will be addressed in the next chapter.

Goals are not written in concrete or unchangeable terms, in fact, as you'll see later on, they should change as your business evolves. But they do give you a starting point and a destination to calibrate to. I always liken having no goals, to turning up at the airport to go on holiday and jumping on the first plane out of there. You might end up in an Icelandic winter with your beach clothes and a fistful of dollars. For some of you, that might sound quite exciting, but if your family suffered as a result, it wouldn't be so much fun.

With this in mind, to achieve your goals, you will have to make some sacrifices in the form of time and energy. This means time otherwise spent with family and the energy to commit to being able to complete them. This is the part that really matters, because it takes a certain type of character to be able to make the choices and sacrifices required, day in and day out, consistently. You'll need to become committed to your plan, be prepared to overcome challenges and work to a strategy, never forgetting that you are ultimately the only one responsible for achieving your outcome. That's right, it's all your fault. Good news and bad news, it's all down to you. As a client said to me recently: "I might be swimming in sh*t, but at least it's my sh*t!"

So how can you gain clarity during the goal setting process? Say I wanted to lose some weight. A simple goal statement like, "I want to lose some weight" is an ambiguous and indefinite statement. It would be more useful if I detailed the amount of weight I wanted to lose and by a specific date. Then I can envisage myself as that person in my mind's eye and what I will look like after reaching my desired outcome. I've suddenly got some clarity on what I need to do and what the end result feels like, and by doing this, it will not only inspire me to lose the weight in the first place, but will also set in motion the necessary habits and sacrifices I'll need to make and give me a real feeling of who I need to become to achieve it.

When we imagine something in detail in our minds, our bodies can't tell the difference between the imagined experience and the real one. The same physiological responses occur in both cases. If you imagine something in detailed Technicolor, your body is literally fooled into thinking it's real. I had a dream recently where I sat on a wasp and it started to chase me. I woke myself up as I tried swatting the wasp away and hit the bedside table. It really looked and felt real - real enough to wake me up. And the bedside table definitely felt real at 3am in the morning! This is because your mind has its very own CGI special effects department to make your imagination and your thinking come to life. How cool is that? Remember, the importance of this exercise is not in the goals themselves, but in the process of planning and the clarity this brings. As Dwight D. Eisenhower said: "In preparing for battle I have always found that plans are useless, but planning is indispensable."

Perhaps you may begin to see why 80% of businesses struggle. Many of them start in the wrong place when it comes to goal setting - and that's if they even do this bit at all. No doubt the majority of them start their business with a plan, yet most still fail and it's because of this simple misunderstanding. They spend too much time on the focus of the plans themselves and not enough time appreciating the planning process itself. They set their sights firmly on the actual goals, whilst missing the most important part of the process, the clarity and insights this exercise brings. If they fail to achieve the specific goal, they feel like a failure, but of course they're missing the point because ultimately, it will be the daily habits and choices you make that will determine your success and these come as a result of getting more clarity on your purpose and really embodying the feeling of success. If you fail to meet a deadline, it doesn't mean you've failed your goal, it just means you didn't make the deadline. As long as you continue the important habits (such as cutting out the donuts to lose weight), you will reach your target eventually.

Bearing in mind what I've just highlighted, another way to turbo charge this part of the process, is to set 'performance goals'. You will then be using the power of compounding (more later) to create a much bigger, but still achievable goal. Performance goals can be controlled by the person who sets the goal, as opposed to outcome goals, which are controlled by others or circumstances outside of our influence. It's best to set performance goals wherever possible in your business, as you are the one in control and these define your ongoing habits. Performance goals focus on your personal performance, while outcome goals focus instead on the results you get.

A team may have an outstanding performance and not win a contest (such as a pitch for a job) because other teams have performed better. Conversely, they may perform poorly and still win, if all other teams perform at a lower level. Outcome goals (results) therefore do not tell the whole story, whereas performance goals are track-able and controllable.

For instance, if your goal is to do one month of worthwhile 90 minute sessions (more on these later) working on your marketing every day, you have far greater control in achieving this, than stating that the end result will be 'a new marketing campaign'. You have even greater control of success if it's done using the correct procedures or habits. In the case of 'worthwhile marketing', turning off all distractions such as email and phones and not being disturbed would assist you greatly. This simple and track-able performance goal gives you more control over your outcome.

There is nothing more discouraging than failing

to achieve a goal for reasons beyond your control. Bad business environments, poor weather, supplier problems, bad luck, bad debt... but at least if you base your goals on personal performance (habits) you can keep control over the achievement of your own targets and the factors that got you there. Who you become from achieving your goal is contained within your performance and this is all ultimately under your own control through your choices.

Examples:

Performance Goal: Create an inspiring 15 min pitch

Outcome Goal: Win the pitch

Performance Goal: Do 90 minutes of marketing every day for a month

Outcome Goal: New marketing campaign

Performance Goal: Make 20 prospecting calls every day for a month

Outcome Goal: Get 100 new customers

Of course, the beauty in this process lies in knowing what is required to achieve the bigger goals. If you know from experience, or from others, that making 20 calls a day for a month will result in around 100 new customers, it's more likely (if you achieve your controllable performance goal), that the outcome goal will also be achieved. By starting the smaller, more achievable performance goal or daily habits, you will start to make inroads into your bigger goal - which, as you might begin to see by now, is actually more of a Trojan horse.

Now that we've gone over some of the basics, we'll get started and create some real life goals, but first, let's do a 'Stock take'.

"Could you tell me the way to Balbriggan, please?"
"You know, if I was going to Balbriggan I wouldn't be starting from here at all…"
- Famous 'Irish Joke'

It's OK, I can include this, as I'm half Irish. A bit tongue in cheek but quite timely for what you're about to create. If you want to know the best pathway between two points, it's all very well knowing where you want to get to, but it's also very useful to know where you are now. I said earlier that I've worked with some businesses who don't know where they are. Well, I exaggerated. Most of the businesses I start working with don't know where they are, so if that's you, you're in good company!

The starting point for everyone I begin coaching, is to get this stock take done, pronto. Let's really see where you are on the map before we start getting ideas about where you want to head and let's begin with some basic questions to find out where you are, by looking first at what you've achieved in the past twelve months:

- What are you most proud of in the past year?
- If there were a broadsheet newspaper headline describing this past twelve months for you, what would it say?
- When were you most excited about life, what were you doing and who were you with?
- Looking back, what (if anything) would you have done differently?
- What new dream did you achieve for yourself?
- Where did you let fear hold you back from a dream or a goal you had?
- What new and inspiring people did you meet in the past year?
- Who do you want to influence you in the year to come?

The reason I'm asking about other people in these last questions is quite simple: research has shown that statistically, you are the 'average' of the five people you spend most time with. Your income will be the average of their incomes. Your values will be the average of their values. Your tastes will be the average of their tastes. So choose wisely who you hang around with! I love this analogy from millionaire entrepreneur Peter Voogd, which sums this up nicely: "If you hang around five confident people, you will be the sixth. If you hang around five intelligent people, you will be the sixth. If you hang around five millionaires, you will be the sixth. If you hang around five idiots, you will be the sixth. If you hang around five broke people, you will be the sixth. It's inevitable."

This is an important part of rethinking your thinking. To be successful, you'll need some more 'success thinking', and hanging around with people who are negative and have defeatest thinking is not going to help you or your business succeed. It's why we are so passionate at the Entrepreneurs Circle about finding the right type of entrepreneurs to have as members within the Circle. Entrepreneurs who believe achieving is inevitable. Those who have the right 'why' to get them motivated. Those who are passionate about making a positive change in the lives of others, because 'Who you hang around with matters, a lot!' (Botty Rule #2: from the book Botty's Rules by The Entrepreneurs Circle's founder and owner, Nigel Botterill).

Next up, we'll look at specific focus areas in your life, which go to make up who you are. As an entrepreneur, your entire life, from your business and personal relationships to your own physical and mental health are just as (if not more) important than any business acumen or skills, because everything you do in life affects everything else. So if you're trying to run a business whilst going through a messy divorce or tackling cancer, it's going to be a lot tougher than if you're living in mental bliss and ultimate health. Put simply, when you feel better, you'll perform better. So how can you go about feeling better on a daily basis?

We'll talk about how you can improve your thinking later on by understanding how the process works, but for now, make a list below of the core areas of your life where you want to get better results and set performance goals: Health; continued learning; helping others; relationships; family; business. These are just some examples, but the more creative you can get, the better. You could say for instance: 'Expand my financial mind by attending a Rich Dad conference' instead of simply 'Continued learning'... or 'I want to bring 1000 children out of poverty in the UK by this time next year'. Anything goes but try not to list any more than five at this point. Although this bit can become quite exciting (and I suggest you do this with your partner and/or family) there is a risk of becoming overwhelmed further down the line if you're too ambitious here or set targets that are simply unattainable.

The idea is to nail the areas in your life that really matter to your business and life success and what that will really look like for you. A good place to start is to think about your life in precisely a year from now. This time next year, what would your life look like if you had achieved exactly what you set out to achieve this year? How would you feel? What would you be doing? Who would you need to become? Sit and imagine your life as if it has already happened and then write down your creative thoughts o.n a piece of paper

Now let's take a look at something that is so important to your success that it deserves some real thinking time. We've touched upon it already but it's really the most vital part of this whole section. Without the right ones, your chances of success are slim to zilch. With the right ones, practised daily, your chances go through the roof. What are we talking about? Your habits, of course!

"We are what we repeatedly do. Excellence, then, is not an act, but a habit." - Aristotle

Start thinking about daily improvements or changes you would like to habitualise in your life. Goals are outcomes you eventually accomplish or can check off your list, whereas habits are behaviours you adopt as a part of your life going forward from here on in. They glue together and compound to make you into the person you need to become to get what you want in life.

Some examples to focus on might be: being early instead of late; scheduling less instead of trying to cram too much in or procrastinating; slowing down and being mindful of situations; spending less time on email or social media (unless it's a part of your marketing strategy of course); simplifying and de-cluttering; eating more healthily; drinking less alcohol or caffeine; exercising more; writing a regular blog or getting a minimum of 8 hours sleep a night; or spending less money on trivial things.

Basically everything you do in life on a regular basis, from your attitude you have when you wake up, to everything you eat and drink, the amount of exercise you choose to do, the way you work, the way you learn... absolutely every behaviour is a result of consistent, continued choices and decisions made over and over again and pieced together to make your life as it is right now.

Everything you see around you in your life is a result of the habits you've chosen on a daily basis. No one else has decided your life for you, no matter how much you want to blame others. The results in your life right now are the results of the choices, which you and you alone have made. If you want to change your life, you'll need to change your habits. It's really very simple in this regard, but then again, changing the habits of a lifetime can be tricky. But it all starts with one word: choice. If you choose to do so, starting right now, then you have a good chance of making this shift happen. As long as the choices you make become consistent, you'll start to build up momentum and make the changes necessary to change your life forever.

The website: 'Zen Habits' has a really effective and simple approach to changing habits - it's best to focus on a maximum of one new habit or resolution at a time (ideally no more than one a month). If you do, or stop doing, this one thing for a month straight, it will likely become a part of your routine. The good news is that for the super ambitious, this allows for 12 new habits in a year!

Here are some simple, easy to implement tips you can make into daily habits, which will transform the way you feel and ultimately lead to peak performance and super high productivity:

- Drink a minimum of 3 litres of water every day
- Go for a short walk daily or a jog, three or four times a week
- Listen to audio books instead of the radio in the car - I cannot tell you how significant this one choice has been in my own life - it's incredible!
- Stop procrastinating by doing focused work in 20 minute chunks instead of getting overwhelmed by big projects and putting them

off to the last minute (OneFocus App works well for this)

- Make a list of tomorrow's tasks every night before you go to sleep, so the next day is already pre-planned
- Write a daily journal including successes and learned lessons from the day's events
- Say "I love you" to your spouse and children every day
- Stop eating junk food - there's nothing more energy sapping than eating a quick fix of processed food or sugar, only to suffer from a massive drop-off soon after
- Stop watching the news - they only seem to cover the cr*p stuff
- Check your Google analytics weekly to know what's really happening on your website and speak with your accountant regularly to know what's happening to the important numbers in your business - you'll be able to make smarter decisions when you know all the facts
- Only drink coffee before 12pm. Coffee is a great anti-oxidant, but drinking too much of it, especially after midday will lead to sleep

deficiency

- And lastly, speaking of which, get to bed by 10pm every night for a minimum of 8 hours' sleep. It's been shown in numerous scientific studies that the main cause of stress, poor performance, and even car accidents is tiredness. Drink less (or zero) alcohol and get to bed early and the next day becomes a breeze

OK, I admit it, these are mine! There are more of these tips in the chapter towards the end of the book about health and life hacks, but I thought it would give you a head start here... so now over to you. Don't forget, everything you do as an entrepreneur is part of who you are and therefore part of your business success going forward., so now it's time to get specific. It's not enough to just say, "I want to be healthier" or "I want to lose weight." Performance goals should be quantifiable and measurable. You can't control whether you actually lose 10 kilos, but you can control what you eat and how often you exercise, which usually leads to losing the weight, so define precisely what you want.

If you want to write a book, then how many words

in a day can you commit to (500 is usually do-able)? List the 'Quantifiable Outcomes and the Specifics' of each goal. This is the part where you'll start to put some 'meat on the bone' as far as the finished picture looks and more importantly, what you'll feel like when you've achieved them. Remember, whatever you imagine needs to feel real, then your body won't be able to tell the difference between the imagined reality and actual reality, and will start to believe it's already happened. Get creative on this part and start to feel like it's already in your life and you'll be making excellent headway into achieving it:

Goal 1: Quantifiable Outcomes and Specifics:
Goal 2: Quantifiable Outcomes and Specifics:
Goal 3: Quantifiable Outcomes and Specifics:

To make sure these goals really happen, you'll need to get some leverage, like the father who couldn't stop smoking until his six-year-old daughter walked into his home office one morning and said, "Daddy, I don't want you to die before I'm 10." He never smoked again!

What vitally important reason can you find for

making your goal an absolute must and doing what is necessary to become the person to achieve it? It could be fitting into a dress for your wedding or being sure you're alive to teach your grandchildren their homework. It's your call but just be sure there is real emotion and meaning behind it.

This part of the process helps to clarify your 'why'. We've already discussed the importance of this earlier on, suffice to say that it's the driving force behind all of your behaviours, which become your habits, which are your choices, which make your successes. So list one 'why' for each goal.

Example:

Goal 1: I want to stop smoking.

Your 'Why': So that I can live to see my daughter get married.

Goal 2: I want to create 10k net profit per month.

Your 'Why': So I have the freedom to spend time watching my children grow up instead of working to make someone else's dreams a reality.

We've already mentioned getting together with friends and family to come up with ideas and plans.

One thing that works really well is getting out of your normal environment with your significant others and really getting clear on your future. Do this regularly and you'll find that the clarity coming from this process really drives you on with your daily habits and success. Victoria and I regularly get together to create vision boards based on the future we want to create. You can use a Pinterest account and keep a board private, but both of you put together images to inspire you into action. One of our members, James Welsh from My Coaching, even has his vision board as framed pictures, and every time he succeeds in one of the areas, he replaces the old image with the real one. The other reason vision boards are so effective is that they are always on display and a good way to remind you why you're putting in the hard work to make them happen. Don't forget, it's the daily habits you undertake and who you become from achieving them that determines your success.

"Great things are not done by impulse, but by a series of small things brought together."
- Vincent Van Gogh

So now it's time to fill in the minor details, or 'Baby Steps' to take next on your journey to entrepreneurial success. As we've already discussed, thinking of a long-term goal as a single item to accomplish can be massively overwhelming. But every goal has all kinds of small tasks leading up to it. Let's say that I want to lose that 10 kilos. My first step would be to go to the kitchen and throw away all the sugary snacks in the cupboard. My second step would be to write down a shopping list of healthy items to get from the stores. My third step would be to go to the shop and buy them, along with a recipe book for healthy eating. This way I am setting myself up for success.

Take each big goal and break it down into 3 to 5 baby steps. You may need more (or fewer) steps depending on the size of your goal.

So for each goal on your list (example):

Big goal: Write a book on my expertise, to amplify my business brand

Step 1: Wake at 6am every day to write a minimum of 500 words
Step 2: Carry a dictaphone everywhere to add

comments and additional resources

Step 3: Post a brief on PeoplePerHour.co.uk to find someone to transcribe my voice notes

Step 4: Go to 99Designs.com to start a cover design process

Step 5: Speak with a book midwife to help with accountability and give me deadlines to reach

This last point is really important. Think about someone who can help you make each goal into a reality. No one does anything entirely on their own and behind every success is a support team who makes it possible. It's precisely why we're here at the EC!

For each of your goals, list one person who could help you achieve it. Ideally they will have experience and expertise on the topic, but this could be someone close to you, a colleague, a friend or even someone you've never met before, but who you'd love to get advice from. List one name for each goal.

Now it's time to get your goals scheduled. Everything we do takes up physical time in our lives. Without putting things on the calendar, it's easy to plan too much or to fill your time with other things. Let's face it, this is going to happen anyway, so you might as well fill it with the steps in your formula.

Look at the goals, habits and resolutions you've created. Begin to place each of them into the weeks and months ahead, ideally on a large wall chart (having them in front of you daily will really help). Be conscious of the time in your life. If you know you'll be traveling throughout November, don't expect huge results that month. If some of your goals will take the whole year to complete, then fill in your minor tasks in the months where you will definitely be able to take action. Just putting this all down on paper will have a huge impact on your chances of making them happen - remember the builder/plan analogy and the clarity this will bring?

If you can get accountable by telling other people about your goals, your chances of success more than treble. We tend to keep our word much better with others than with ourselves. Pick at least three people close to you to tell about your goals and deadlines. They'll be your 'accountability allies'. Walk them through your process. Explain why it's important to you and give them a copy of your goals and plans. Write down who your accountability ally will be and what they can do to keep you accountable. Perhaps suggest the process you went through with them too and get them to create some goals of their own so you can help each other.

To see progress, you should keep your plans front of mind by creating a routine that allows you to review your tasks on a weekly basis. Dreams become reality when you consistently address them and make small gradual progress. The compound effect will ensure that within a year, your achievements can become a reality, but more importantly, you will become the person you need to achieve them.

Now that you have your goals and steps written down, I want you to do one last thing which will turbo-charge your success: Do something... right now!!

"Never leave the site of setting a goal without first taking some form of positive action toward its attainment" - Tony Robbins

It could be the tiniest thing in the world. Maybe send a short email or make a quick list, make a post of your intention on social media or call a friend to let them know. Pick something that only takes 5 minutes or less, but do it now! I regularly do Goal Setting workshops at the Entrepreneurs Circle's National Support Centre in Birmingham and getting attendees to do this one last step is often the exercise that really makes the difference. Just by starting, you'll set the wheels in motion which will get you motoring towards your self-created future, and as every journey starts with a single step, now's the time to take yours.

Well done! The fact that you've finished this process means you've got some clarity. Now all you need is the final ingredient; persistence. We constantly stress the importance of the word 'implementation' within the Entrepreneurs Circle, because unless you actually do it, nothing will happen. Dreams don't become reality simply by dreaming about them. The magic happens when a consistent process of dedicated action is applied to the things that matter most in your life, and make no mistake, hard work is required.

"A dream doesn't become reality through magic; it takes sweat, determination and hard work"
- Colin Powell

When you get committed on the level we've just gone to, the sky (or your imagination) is the limit. This is what has turned the impossible into the possible for me and many other entrepreneurs and is what makes the difference between a life of mediocrity and a super successful one. We all have a lot more power than we often give ourselves credit for. All we have to do is want it badly enough, start the journey and be consistent. That part is up to you, but here's to a year of doing what actually matters - to you and your super success in achieving your goals for your business, your family and your life.

CASE STUDY: BARRY ALLAWAY, MANAGING DIRECTOR AT WORLDWIDE MAGAZINE DISTRIBUTION (WWMD)

This year I've launched three information products, created a global magazine consultancy service, supported my private clients, as well as doing all the day-to-day stuff that's allowed WWMD to buck the trend and continue to grow in a market that's declining. In addition, I'm heavily involved in charity work, I help my teenage boys run their craft stall at the weekends, and I run a number of business projects in my own time.

I don't have any more time than the average person, in fact you could say that I'm more challenged than most! My wife, Hazel calls me a 'restless visionary'. I'm continually looking at what I can do next and as such, I needed to create a system that would allow me to implement as quickly as my imagination conjures up new ideas.

'Setting' a goal is far too much about the intention and less about the actual implementation. After all a 'set' goal makes no impact on your business or your life until it's a tangible reality. And that's why I'm a huge advocate for goal 'getting'.

I always start the process from a positive perspective. This positive focus is a great method of helping me to cut through any self doubt and to think big. I make a list of my achievements (both personally and professionally) and keep topping up the tally.

With this positive mindset in place, my next step is to think about the next 90 days and what is most important to me. I usually take a day out of the business to do this and get clear on what needs my urgent attention. For example: Is there a threat I must overcome or a need to respond to market pressures? Is there a large project I want to deliver that I feel is going to make a big wave in my business? My secret here is to focus on the pressing priorities of the here and now - not what I thought would matter when I crafted a five year plan three years ago!

Times change fast and this cutting edge focus means I'm always pushing forward with the most relevant plans and projects - and realising the benefits of their implementation with optimal timing.

Then I break each objective down into bite size chunks. Once I've identified the three or four key projects that are going to get my focus over the following 90 days, my next step is to break them down into easy to implement tasks.

Then I schedule time in my diary where I'll attack each task. This day-to-day progress keeps me tightly focused and on track and drives the momentum needed to make the delivery of a big project less daunting.

I've found that the best way to implement the tasks is to aim for 90 minutes of focused activity each day. I protect this time religiously and schedule it into my diary. People know not to disturb me and it works. I get loads done, but more importantly I still have plenty of time for all the day-to-day stuff and my core business is not compromised by the extra activity. In fact, it's hugely enhanced.

When I come to the end of the 90 days, I review what's worked and what hasn't - in preparation to start the cycle again. The review is so valuable because you discover very quickly if an idea will have the impact you anticipated. If it has, then brilliant, but if not, the time wasted was minimal. What's more, I've always learnt something valuable that allows me to attack the next set of 90 day priorities with fresh insight. This system works brilliantly for me (and for others) because it helps me deliver the projects that build success.

wwmd.co.uk

"Between stimulus and response there is a space. In that space is our power to choose our response. In our response lies our growth and our freedom."

\- Viktor E. Frankl

ELEMENT THREE:
OVERCOMING FEAR: THE ENTREPRENEUR MINDSET AND EFFECTIVE DECISION MAKING

"People who don't take step number one, never ever take step number two" - Zig Zigler

It's at this point that many other books or courses might leave you to your own devices. After all, you've got your 'why' and some clarity on your goals, and even read case studies from business owners who've achieved excellent results by breaking these down into smaller chunks and consistently implementing the necessary habits. So what else do you need to get started?

Well, quite a lot as it goes. You see, most budding entrepreneurs get a boost from defining their 'why', goals and habits, but falter somewhere further down the line due to procrastination, feeling overwhelmed, or having a crippling fear of failure. Whether it's direct fear of failing or a fear of success, fears passed down from your peers or even learned fears - this chapter is all about how you can overcome them and clear your path to entrepreneurial success. This chapter is actually all about you!Everyone at one stage or another has had a fear of something. Although we're born with only two innate fears, the fear of falling and loud noises, we inherit all of the others, which is great news, because that means we can un-inherit them too!

In your life up to this point, what have you given up or missed out on due to having a fear of one form or another? What have you stopped doing or perhaps not even started doing due to fearful thinking? Notice I'm pinpointing 'thinking' here as the culprit early on, because it's your thinking that prescribes your daily actions and habits, and in this chapter we're going to delve into what you can do with your thinking to create the 'Entrepreneur Success Mindset'.

The most successful entrepreneurs throughout history, from Andrew Carnegie to Thomas Edison, Henry Ford to Ray Kroc, Steve Jobs to Bill Gates, and Jeff Bezos to Sir Richard Branson, all had (and some still do of course) a way of thinking that allowed them to 'get things done' more effectively.

In his superb book The 7 Day Start-up, Dan Norris develops this mindset through having to launch a business out of sheer necessity in just seven days. There was simply no time to sit and think, it just had to happen. And the results were incredible. He made more money in those seven days than in any of his other launch ventures combined. He wasn't allowed to ruminate and cogitate, he just had to do it.

OK, it's unlikely you will ever be in a position where you have no alternative but to bypass your self-sabotaging thinking, so how can you, as an entrepreneur, tap into this 'success thinking' of some of the greatest business people who've ever lived? Well, this chapter is not about how to use visualisation or self-hypnosis. Nor is it about relaxation techniques or self-esteem boosting strategies. While these approaches can give you temporary relief from fear, anxiety and self-doubt in the short term, they rarely give you genuine confidence in the long term. This chapter is also not going to be about strategies, tips or tricks to get you thinking straight. Why not? Because they are based on the wrong rules of the game.

"You have to learn the rules of the game.
And then you have to play better than anyone else"
- Albert Einstein

So what are the rules of the game? What is it that these successful business owners knew that we don't? Put simply, they did what was necessary without their thinking sabotaging their behaviours. I'm going to repeat this because it's very, very important. They did what was necessary without their thinking sabotaging their behaviours.

They were able to action what was necessary for success, without fear taking over and charting a different course. If you spend time reading about these visionaries, you'll begin to spot the patterns. They definitely took risks. They definitely made mistakes, but it didn't deter them. In fact it seemed to spur them onto more action, not less. They realised that 'failure' was actually part of the process and a requirement, rather than something to be avoided. They actually embraced it!

We're living in a society today where danger is supposedly everywhere. If you watch the news, all you see is horror stories and fear inducing nonsense. Our own parents tried to protect us from an early age and did everything they could to keep us safe from harm. But as soon as we were exposed to anything remotely dangerous, they interjected without allowing us to experience it for ourselves. And yet we did fall over when we started to walk. Sometimes it hurt. But we never gave up. It was this 'learning' that sparked the alterations and adjustments required to make walking possible. We had no choice but to carry on, so we did. Do you see where this and Dan Norris's 'Seven Day Start-up' example match up? When we have no other options, we do, regardless. When we somehow manage to utilise this fearful thinking, actions become easier. But not just any actions, we're talking inspired, insightful actions here. When we connect to clarity and insightful thinking, rather than our own personal, fearful thinking, we are destined for success. How can we do this on a regular basis?

Well, as with most things in life, when we understand how it works, it's easier to utilise. Think of the last time you conquered some complicated software. The same applies to our own thinking. When we understand how it actually works, instead of how we believe it works, we get to play the game better than anyone else. So what you are about to hear might sound rather counter-intuitive, but I assure you it's going to make a huge difference in your life and in your business. It's actually the reason why I can now walk on stage in front of thousands of people and deliver talks and training, when only a few years ago I suffered from crippling OCD (Obsessive Compulsive Disorder) and would struggle to leave the house let alone speak publicly.

Only five years ago, I believed that if I didn't touch certain objects in a certain way before I left any room, my entire family would die! I also had a nervous squint, which was rather embarrassing, but in both cases, I was being fooled by my own thinking. Nothing else, just my thinking. How do I know? Well, many years later and there are now thousands of times when I haven't gone through the same routine, and my family are still alive and well. I now realise that these perceived consequences of my fearful thinking were coming from me, and not from outside of me. This is very similar in fact to any sort of fearful thinking, worry, anxiety and concerns about life. Although this seems obvious upon reflection, it is actually pointing to a deeper truth, which affects everyone and will help you in your entrepreneurial journey. It's actually part of the building blocks of all success and part of a system which every living being is using to function, whether they know it or not. When I learned these rules of the game, it made it so much easier to play, and put quite simply, the rules of the game are as follows:

We all create our own version of life (our reality), via the gift of thought - from the 'inside-out' and not from the 'outside-in'. To have any reality whatsoever, it has to come via a thought and can only come through, or via our thinking. This means that although it looks like we experience life as a result of what is happening to us, this is actually not true. It HAS to come from us first. This very simple understanding will help you to deal with all sorts of problems in your entrepreneurial journey, because when you see where your feelings are actually coming from - your own thinking – you'll have the ability to respond to them (response-ability) in infinite ways, instead of just one. In addition, there is a source of well being and insight available to everyone at all times and we can see this more clearly when our personal thinking subsides and wisdom emerges.

That's it. Told you it was simple. All fearful thinking is self-created, and as such is within your own control. You might well be thinking right now that this can't be true. After all, if I dropped a tarantula in your lap,

surely the fear you feel would have been created by
my actions. Well, yes... and no. You see, although my
actions have led to a circumstance in which I have put
your life in apparent danger, and you'd be sensible
to fear for your life, the feelings you are immersed in
are still being created by you and not by the spider, or
indeed me. How can this be true?

Well if I gave the same furry arachnid to my two
year old daughter Annie-Rose for instance, she'd try
and hug it! It's only your own thinking that makes it
into a fearful situation. Sometimes it's very useful to
have a fight, flight or freeze response. It might be more
useful for Annie-Rose to retreat or freeze than to hug
it, but she's just such a huggy little baby and simply
adores pets (not that I would ever give her a venomous
spider as a pet, I should just add!).

This one simple rule of the game allowed me to
see that it was me, sabotaging myself through my
own thinking, and as soon as I woke up to this truth,
I simply stopped doing it. It no longer made sense
for me to do it, so I stopped. Kind of like having a
throbbing headache and then realising you've been
hitting yourself on the head with a large frying pan.
As soon as you see this as the source of your pain,

you don't have to try alternative hitting techniques... you just stop hitting. Now even this example requires further analysis, because some people might not regard this pain as unpleasant. Some people might even pay for it!

Whatever type of thinking we have about anything, results in a corresponding feeling. What we think, is what we feel - but we're doing it to ourselves, because it's coming from us. When we see that we are the ones creating our reality via our thinking, we also get to see that fearful thinking preventing us from doing what it takes to be successful (ie: by making mistakes and learning from them) is not useful. We get to see how the rules work and we get to play by different rules. We see that it's not useful, so we stop doing it. Seeing that we are the creators of our reality via our thinking allows us to step back and wait for more insightful thoughts to emerge - the sort of thinking that gave us the inkling to take the risk of entrepreneurship in the first place and just felt right. The clarity and insight thinking that has been urging you to make your "Dent on the Universe" as Steve Jobs puts it.

We're not talking about 'changing your thinking' here. That's something that often comes up from participants in my training workshops. That's akin to altering the way you hit yourself on the head with the frying pan. When you see that it's your thinking doing the damage, there's less need to do anything... it's just a thought, after all. The same applies for 'positive thinking'. If you believe that your well being comes from your thinking, you'll spend a lot of time and energy trying to think positively. But your well being does not come from your thinking. It comes from something beyond you. You are not your thoughts... you are the one observing thought.

I love the analogy that Andy McNab, the former SAS soldier writes in his book 'The Good Psychopath's Guide to Success', when he describes our lives as a movie and our feelings as the accompanying soundtrack. Without the music, no matter what we see on screen, there is less feeling involved when we turn down or delete the sound. But the movie always carries on regardless. The same is true in life. It's going to carry on regardless of the feelings you are having about it. And your feelings are being created by your thinking, every time.

When you see the power your thinking has held over you in the past and you have the realisation that this is only thought, something marvellous happens. Like dressing a shadow, you see the pointless nature of getting fooled by it again. You see it for what it is. Just a thought. Another thought then replaces the old one. Like clouds in the sky, new thinking is always going to replace old thinking so long as we don't get involved in the process. The system is designed to clear away the old thinking and replace it with fresh, new thinking. If you let the system do the heavy lifting, it takes a lot less energy than trying to change the thinking yourself. This approach to understanding the inside out nature of experience through how our thinking actually works, is based on the Three Principles of Mind, Consciousness and Thought uncovered by the late Sydney Banks.

I hope this is starting to make some sense? It's a very different way of approaching this subject, but it's proving incredibly useful for many successful business owners who've been introduced to this new path to understanding their own thought processes. One client in particular, who'd been crippled by fear for years and had a stagnated business as a result, managed to achieve more in the space of a few weeks after realising that her own thinking was the cause of the sabotage preventing her from taking the inspired action required for success. Just seeing how the system worked allowed her to notice what was true and what was her own fearful thinking. This realisation gave her the opportunity to ignore the fearful thoughts and take action on the insightful ones instead.

When we see how the system is actually working, it makes it so much easier to embrace failure, like our super successful entrepreneurs, because we know that the feelings we are getting are as a result of our thinking and not the external event. The lessons learned by failure are not only useful, but need to be allowed in and embraced, and without our personal thinking sabotaging us, we can get on with the journey using our new found knowledge to adjust course.

For instance, if you were able to ignore fearful thinking, what sort of things would you do and what sort of person would you be?

- How would you behave differently?
- How would you walk and talk differently?
- How would you play, work and perform differently?
- How would you treat others differently: your friends, relatives, partner, parents, children and

work colleagues?

- How would you treat yourself differently?
- How would your character change?
- What would you stop doing?

Failure is a necessary part of life and fundamental to the process in learning how to succeed. It's part of how we became to be the most successful living creatures in the entire Universe (as far as we know). Our whole evolutionary process is based on failure. Failure of genetic mutations leads to the success of others. Without failure, we actually cease to grow.

Thomas Edison is famously quoted as saying: 'I have not failed. I've just found 10,000 ways that won't work.' He also said: 'Our greatest weakness lies in giving up. The most certain way to succeed is always to try just one more time.' There is immense power in these words, not least because they come from a man who changed the world with his inventions: the electric light bulb, the phonograph and motion picture camera. This was a man who, when his entire factory was burning to the ground (which set him back years and cost him millions of dollars) told his eldest son to "Go get your mother and all her friends. They'll never see a fire like this again"! He used this incredible failure as the impetus to start all over again.

We can't change the fact that adverse things will sometimes happen to us. We can however change how we react to them. It's not how many times you fall over that matters; it's how many times you get back up! In the book, *The Obstacle Is the Way: The Timeless Art of Turning Trials into Triumph*, author Ryan Holiday says that Edison could have wept, yelled in anger, or locked himself in his house in a state of depression. But instead, he put on a smile and told his son to enjoy the spectacle. "To do great things, we need to be able to endure tragedy and setbacks," Holiday writes. "We've got to love what we do and all that it entails, good and bad."

We should therefore all be treating failure as one of the most, if not the most important and essential elements in the success formula and actually be trying to fail more often, not less. There are so many more examples of failure from super successful entrepreneurs, so let's list a few now:

- Walt Disney's first animation studio, 'Iwerks-Disney Commercial Artists', went bust after just one month

- Oprah Winfrey lost her job as news anchor on WJZ-TV in Baltimore when they told her that she 'wasn't fit for television'
- Albert Einstein wanted to attend the prestigious Swiss Polytechnic Institute, but he did not even pass the entrance examination!
- Steven Spielberg applied to the University of Southern California School of Theater, Film and Television on three separate occasions - but each time he was unsuccessful because of his C grade average
- The first business venture of Microsoft co-founders Bill Gates and Paul Allen was called 'Traf-O-Data' and it flopped miserably
- Abraham Lincoln was defeated in his first bid for a seat in the Illinois House of Representatives. So he opened a general store but within a few months, it went bust
- Ernest Hemingway, one of the greatest writers of the twentieth century said: "The first draft of anything... is sh*t."
- Thomas Watson, president of IBM, when asked, "What is the formula for success?" replied:

"Double your rate of failure."

- The best basketball player who's ever lived, Michael Jordan, failed to even make it into his high school basketball team! Speaking about his incredible career, he said: "I've missed more than 9,000 shots in my career. I've lost almost 300 games. Twenty-six times I've been trusted to take the game winning shot... and missed. I've failed over and over and over again in my life and that is why I succeed."

In other words, in learning to do anything well, we're going to make plenty of mistakes and have to overcome some pretty big challenges along the way. And the further we venture into uncharted waters, the more likely we are going to screw up. Accept and embrace failure as an essential part of your journey, you'll be much better off than if you fight against it.

"Success is the ability to go from failure to failure without loss of enthusiasm." - Sir Winston Churchill

Consider the following conundrum: Q: What is the biggest cause of failure in business? A: Inaction, due to a fear of failure. Q: What is the biggest cause of success in business? A: Lessons learned from massive failure. Oh the irony!

Our thoughts play the most important role in creating, maintaining and exacerbating fears, and the best way to deal with these is through understanding the process and how these manifest into the feelings of fear.

So what exactly are thoughts? Put simply, thoughts are the words and pictures inside your head. We don't notice all of our thoughts and many are sub, or unconscious, such as the thought to make your body sweat, cuts heal, your heartbeat, or your lungs inflate. Memories, beliefs, attitudes, assumptions, values, dreams, desires and judgments are all conscious thoughts... but they are all constructed from two basic building blocks: words and images.

If you close your eyes right now and notice what your mind is doing, you may notice words - which you may hear like a voice or see written images - or pictures, or even a combination of both. If your mind goes blank, just wait... it won't take long before it says something like 'I'm not having any thoughts' - which is, of course, a thought.

If you only noticed feelings in your body and no words or pictures inside your head, these feelings also came from a thought. It's actually not possible to have a feeling without having a thought first. In my book: Do Nothing! I discuss a condition called Congenital Insensitivity to Pain or Congenital Analgesia, where the sufferers cannot feel pain due to a malfunction of the SCN9A gene. There is no thought telling them that their hand is immersed in boiling water, so they cannot feel their own skin melting. No thought, no feeling, no reality... for them.

Consider for a moment how many thoughts your mind creates in the course of a day. On average, and according to experiments - it's around 70-80 thousand. The mind will always give you something to say, or something to show you. As long as you're alive, this process is working for you.

You've probably also noticed that your mind can be a bit negative sometimes. This is perfectly natural and normal. Although the human mind is quick to judge and criticise (you may know someone personally who always points out what's not good enough), the fact is this that the human mind has evolved to think negatively and to fully understand why this is, we need to look at our primitive ancestors.

A hundred thousand years ago, we had four basic needs: food, water, shelter and to continue our own gene survival, none of which is very important... if you're dead! Back then, the number one job that your thinking had to deal with (more than any other) was to not get killed. How does a mind do that then? Well it looks around for danger, constantly scanning the environment and trying to spot or anticipate anything that can possibly hurt you.

A hundred thousand years ago, if your mind was not very good at doing just this one thing, then you didn't live very long and your genes stopped. There was no shortage of violent ways to die, not least the seismic shifts in the earth and the resulting earthquakes and volcanoes, let alone the risk of disease or getting eaten by wild beasts! So if there ever was an early human who went through life in a fearless and carefree manner, only noticing all the wonderful things around them, thinking positively that nothing would ever go wrong, they would have been eaten, burned or murdered pretty quickly - long before they had a chance to reproduce.

We evolved from the ancestors who were always on

the lookout for danger and always had to be prepared for the worst, so our modern brains are always trying to anticipate what could hurt or harm us; always trying to predict what might go wrong. It's no wonder we all have so many doubts, worries, concerns and fears. This is therefore not a sign of a weak or defective mind; but a perfectly natural by-product of evolution and that is why, even if we are told to diligently practice 'positive thinking every single day of our lives, we simply can't stop our minds from generating negative thoughts from time to time. Thoughts are like the clouds in the sky, another one will be along in a minute, and try as we might to change the weather, we simply can't - it's pointless, a waste of good energy. Nature will always win that battle.

Although our minds are perfectly enabled for us to make incredible leaps forward in technology, to walk on the moon and discover new vaccines, they are also hard-wired to criticise and judge - to conjure up scary stories about the future, and dredge up painful memories from the past. There is absolutely nothing wrong with this. These functions are the ordinary processes of a normal, healthy human mind.

As soon as we even think about stepping out of

our comfort zones, our minds will start telling us the same old stories we've been hearing since we were young (and may still be hearing from family and friends now!). 'You'll mess this up', 'You're not good enough', or 'It's way too hard, get a job'. We can either believe these thoughts as truth and tell ourselves: 'I can't do it', or we can challenge the thoughts, and look for evidence that they're not actually true. We can try to replace them with more positive thoughts or distract ourselves from them. You may like to try these things out if you've never done so before. However, if you have tried them already, you might have recognised that they require a lot of effort and energy: even if they do give you temporary relief from the negative thoughts. Your mind just keeps on coming up with new ones: and when you leave your comfort zone to enter a genuinely challenging situation, these techniques don't help you at all.

Instead, re-read this chapter from the beginning and ask yourself the following question: Are negative thoughts really that much of a problem? They are, after all... just thoughts. As someone who had OCD, I know that sufferers have recurrent negative thoughts many times a day. They imagine or worry that all sorts of really bad things will happen - 'My house will burn down', or 'My children will die' - if I don't do this thing. They get very distressed by these thoughts and are often totally convinced that they will come true. But they start to recover when they realise that these thoughts are not actually real. Sufferers have typically had these negative thoughts many thousands of times - totally and utterly believing them - and yet they have never manifested in reality.

Another common belief is that negative thoughts are problematic because 'our thoughts control our actions'. If this were true, the human race would be in really serious trouble. After all, how often have you been so mad at somebody you care about, that you thought about hurting them in some way - yelling at them, shaking them, leaving them or 'getting your own back'? Be honest with yourself; we've all have these thoughts at times. Now just imagine if those thoughts had actually controlled you; if you had actually gone and done all those hurtful things. What would have happened to your closest relationships? Would you still have any friends left?! Have you ever thought about quitting, yet persisted? Have you ever thought of running away, but stayed and stuck it out? Our thoughts don't control our actions because we have the gift of freewill to decide which thoughts we act upon.

So we're not going to reduce, challenge, eliminate or change negative thoughts because we're going to start from the assumption that negative thoughts are not inherently problematic, they are after-all... just thoughts. It's not even about whether our thoughts are true or false, it's about whether they're helpful or not. If we allow these thoughts to guide our actions, will they help us to achieve the results we want? Will they help us to make decisions, to be the person we want to be? Will they help us to create the life we want to live?

When we run away, withdraw or hide from our challenges, it looks like we are somehow at the mercy of our emotions - which control our every move - but this fear of fear itself creates the illusion that our strong emotions are somehow dangerous, which in turn feeds the myth that we can't act the way we want to unless we can control the way we feel. This is a misunderstanding of how thought works.

Under most circumstances, fear is an unpleasant feeling. I say 'most circumstances' because it's not unknown for people to spend good money on being scared out of their wits. I took a ride on the Tower of

Terror once in Disneyland, Paris. I'd do it again in an instant. I loved it! But given that fear usually feels unpleasant, it's only natural we should try to avoid or get rid of it entirely. This method of dealing with the feelings is called 'avoidance'. We distract ourselves by doing anything other than the task at hand. We read books, go to the movies, surf the internet, chat with friends, clean the house, over-eat, drink too much. The more we invest our time and energy in anything else to distract us from 'those feelings', the less time and energy we invest in the things that really matter, and to avoid uncomfortable feelings, we opt out of challenging situations entirely. We withdraw, procrastinate, stay away from people, places and events, or activities, and the more we use this as a strategy for avoiding fear, the smaller our lives become. But here's the real kicker. Fear cannot exist in the present. It only exists in our imaginations of a future, which has not happened yet. When we avoid taking risks or we avoid stepping out of our comfort zone, or facing our challenges, we are actually missing out on life itself.

It's been shown that 96% of our thinking is in either the past or the future... not in the present! How amazing is that; all we have is the present and we spend so little time actually here!

One much talked about technique of opting out, is of course, procrastination - putting things off until later to avoid the pain in the present moment or facing a possibility that we are unable to live up to the task. If we procrastinate too much, important issues are avoided, problems do not get resolved, and our 'to-do' list grows bigger and bigger (generating additional anxious thinking).

And then there's substance abuse. From time to time, we all put substances into our bodies in an attempt to get rid of unpleasant feelings and/ or replace them with more pleasant ones. Tea or coffee, prescription medications, alcohol, tobacco, marijuana or other illicit drugs, chocolate, pizza, ice cream, hamburgers or chips... If we over-rely on any substance use, the costs to our physical health varies from addiction to lung cancer to obesity.

But the biggest cost of all of these strategies and tactics is that the more we avoid our own fear (thoughts), the bigger they grow as something that is not real and the more influence they have over our actions. We get stuck in a fear trap and the greater our efforts to get rid of the fear, the greater our fear becomes, and the more negatively it affects our lives. Can you see why knowing the rules of the game are so important? Just knowing where these feelings are really coming from and what they mean gives me back all of the power to do something about it. I have the 'response-ability' back.

Now despite me knowing that fearful thoughts are coming from me and are just thought, they still arise in certain circumstances. But instead of trying to block them out or change them, it's so much more useful for me to engage with the power of this awesome system and utilise them. So let's take public speaking as an example.

When I went on stage at the National conference at the ICC in Birmingham in 2014, in front of 1,200 people, it looked as if I was taking a stroll in the park. At least that's what members told me afterwards. Of course, what they didn't see was that backstage, just prior to walking on calmly, I was jumping up and down like an over-excited Tigger from Winnie the Pooh! And no matter how good my understanding of how thought works, it's not going to stop thought from continuing to come through me. So yes, I had thoughts of 'what if

I forget something?' and 'what if my slides fail?', but I know now to not to pay attention to them if I don't want to. You don't ever have to actually believe your thinking. Instead, it occurred to me that the feelings I had were those of excitement about how much I was looking forward to sharing my knowledge with so many wonderful people. Instead of giving into fearful thinking, I harnessed those excited feelings (thoughts) and channeled them through me - which made me want to jump up and down in sheer excitement. Fear... is therefore excitement without the breath.

Suppose you too could defuse from all those thoughts you have about how bad or unpleasant your fear is around public speaking, and how much you dislike the thought of it (if you do that is - I happen to love it now). But instead of trying to make the thoughts go away or make them positive, you non-judgmentally notice the physical sensations attached to them. As we've already seen, trying to get rid of your fearful thoughts takes up a lot of energy and is very distracting - and it's hard to engage fully in your life while you're busy struggling with this.

A study in 1988 by psychologists AR Rich and DK Woolever showed that students sitting academic tests, who could engage fully in the exam, instead of getting distracted by their own thoughts and feelings, performed well, no matter how anxious they were prior to taking the exam.

When you unhook from 'changing your thoughts' but instead make space for the unpleasant feelings to come through you and then engage fully in the task you are doing, knowing that thoughts are harmless - you will perform well, regardless of how anxious you feel at the time. Furthermore, the energy that you once spent on struggling with fear and trying to do something about it, can now be invested in taking effective action instead.

So if we know how to harness this powerful energy, we can use it to our advantage, but if we don't know how to handle it, we get into trouble. Imagine approaching a wild stallion without some good horse handling skills: you'd get kicked, bitten or trampled and waste a lot of time and energy in the process. On the other hand, if you're a skilled horse-whisperer, then you know how to approach it safely. Over time, if you treat it well, you can build a good relationship and ride it.

When fear shows up, you know it's there, as the

feelings inside will tell you, but this is being generated by your own thinking, remember that. Instead, feel those strong emotions and intense swirling feelings inside and become more aware of them and how they are moving around. Imagine that wild stallion racing around inside of you. If you ever want to make use of its awesome strength, speed and stamina, you first have to allow it to stay on your land. The same goes for fear.

There is incredible energy in fear, which has evolved over hundreds of millions of years to prepare our bodies for action. The heightened awareness and greater strength it gives us is like rocket fuel and we should learn how to use it to our advantage. When you feel adrenaline flowing through your body, ask yourself 'How can I make use of all this incredibly powerful energy?'

In any new situation, regardless of whether or not we feel confident, we will always feel some amount of fear. It's basic human biology, so when we're facing a new and genuine challenge, we're going to have some sort of fight-or-flight response. It's our mind's way of deciding to stay, or get the hell out of there. No matter how confident we are at doing something new or difficult - if the situation is challenging - we'll feel fear. Fearlessness is therefore not the absence of fear; it is our transformed relationship with fearful thinking.

Make room for the fear, notice it, allow it, channel it... and now take a deep breath, and say to yourself, 'Okay! Here we go! Let's put this incredible energy into action!' The fear is still there, but your relationship with it has transformed. You can then do the same thing in all aspects of your life.

The key then to peak performance is being able to totally engage in the task. I've worked with athletes who call it 'being in the zone'. My partner Victoria calls it 'allowing flow' - total absorption in the task at hand. Time seems to stop dead. There is no internal commentary and nothing distracts us as our bodies and minds work in perfect harmony together. It is in this state that peak performance happens. We have allowed our personal thinking to come through us with no blockages. Not interfering with the natural process makes space for clarity and insightful thinking to emerge.

What we have touched upon here is a totally different approach to the fearful thinking which prevents us from taking inspired action. This is an approach that is in harmony with the system itself, rather than one which needs changing, altering, adjusting or stopping entirely. And the best thing about this new way of approaching fearful thought is that, because it is totally in harmony with the way the system is designed to work, it allows the most incredible and powerful part of the whole process the space to really work its magic. What part is this? Our own built in connection to the answers we already need:

"It is always with excitement that I wake up in the morning wondering what my intuition will toss up to me, like gifts from the sea. I work with it and rely on it. It's my partner." Jonas Salk was the discoverer and developer of the Polio vaccine. In 1957, polio was considered one of the most frightening public health problems in the world. Epidemics were on the increase in America in particular and apart from the atomic bomb, the public's greatest fear was polio. Jonas Salk worked tirelessly to discover a vaccine that would rid the world of this paralysing plague. "Intuition will tell the thinking mind where to look next" he said as he edged closer and closer to finding a cure. He imagined himself as the virus and what it would feel like to be healthy, and with this imagination and trust in his own intuition, on July 2, 1952, Salk injected 43 children with a 'killed-virus' vaccine. A few weeks later at a conference in New York, he announced that his wife and three sons had been among the first volunteers to be inoculated with the vaccine. Thousands upon thousands of successful field trials followed and on April 12, 1955, Dr. Thomas Francis of the University of Michigan declared the vaccine to be safe and effective. By the time Dr Francis stepped down from the podium, church bells were ringing across the country, synagogues and churches were holding prayer meetings of thanks, and parents and teachers were weeping, as if a war had ended.

There will almost certainly be times in your own journey when there will be big decisions to make, and although all the evidence is pointing towards you taking one option, your intuition may be telling you otherwise, which option do you take in these scenarios? Well, what I can tell you from years and years of experience working with business owners, is that your intuition is rarely wrong. It's just that we don't often listen to it. In fact, it's always there telling us the way to go, if only we listen carefully enough.

One of the courses I run for the Entrepreneurs

Circle is called 'The Will 2 Act' and involves in-depth discussions into where intuition, wisdom and clarity of thought come from. One business owner who attended the day wasn't totally sure what we were pointing to during the course, but sent me an email the following day describing a situation that occurred on his way home. As he was driving down the motorway at 80mph, he had a sense that there was something wrong. He pulled into the motorway services and looked over his car thoroughly but couldn't find anything wrong. However, he'd taken on board the discussions during the day and decided to trust his intuition and drive home carefully on the longer country roads, instead of the motorway. As he drove around a long bend on a B-road, the bottom end of his car collapsed. Had he been driving full-pelt down the motorway, he would almost certainly have been killed.

I've had circumstances where my own little 'voice of wisdom' has told me to do something out of the ordinary, like also taking a longer route somewhere, only to find when I arrive that there was a pile-up on the other route just at the time I was going to be there.

It's that same little voice that tells you where your car keys are when you've exhausted going to the drawer for the 17th time expecting them to suddenly appear out of nowhere. It's the same little voice that tells you not to send that fiercely written email response; the one telling you to go home and get some sleep, instead of staying for that 'one more drink'.

We're always connected to it, because it's part of our very nature. To say we're disconnected from it, would be like saying a water droplet is not part of the ocean. And we can access it whenever we wish. Even in the darkest of times, which may perhaps sound strange.

After all, I'm reckoning that some of you might have read that last paragraph and thoughts of practicing meditation or having a still, quiet mind, may have popped into your head. Although it's certainly easier to make decisions when our heads are still and clear and free from distraction, this isn't essential. In fact, I've worked with people who've told me how they've accessed this clarity of thought, insight and wisdom at precisely the time that they would have been panicking. Like the basketball player who had to make a winning three point throw with only two seconds on the clock and 28,000 spectators cheering in his ears, only to describe how it felt as if the entire stadium went silent and he was completely 'at one' with the court and ball. Being in the zone doesn't take sitting lotus position in a quiet room to be able to access it.

Another graphic example of this permanent connection to wisdom happened in the Nairobi shopping hijack where a group of terrorists took siege of a shopping centre in the city and started indiscriminately killing families. We can't even begin to imagine what sort of insane thoughts were going through the heads of the perpetrators of this act at that time, but whatever they were, they must have made sense to those who carried out the atrocities. And yet, when a four year old British boy, Elliot Prior confronted one of the attackers, who'd just shot his Mother who lay bleeding, and told him "Stop shooting, you're a very bad man," this terrorist, even in the midst of his own utterly insane thinking, was able to reconnect to his own wisdom and told the boy: "Forgive us, we are not monsters." He then gave the boy some chocolate and set his family free. There's nothing we need to do to access this clarity of thought. It's always with us, hiding in plain sight, but we do tend to pay attention to it when we have less on our minds.

When asked where they got their problem solving

thinking from, a recent survey of leading company executives came up with some strikingly similar answers: "In the shower," "On the golf course," "When I'm taking the dog for a walk," "Whilst shaving," "Driving the car." In fact, just about everywhere apart from in the office, staring at the problem itself! It's no wonder that Friedrich Nietzsche said: "All truly great thoughts are conceived by walking" and Albert Einstein added: "We cannot solve our problems with the same thinking we used when we created them." When we're looking towards techniques to make better decisions, we're overlooking the most powerful and easily accessible resource available to us all. Our own wisdom and insight is always there, always working and always free, but for our own personal thinking blocking the flow.

I hope this chapter has been helpful in pointing you towards a new approach in dealing with fearful thinking and making effective decisions. In the next chapter, we're going to unravel more unhelpful thinking about what it takes to set up a business in the first place and address how to get a stack full of customers beating a path to your door in the process.

CASE STUDY: EUGENIE VERNEY, BUSINESS COMMUNICATIONS STRATEGIST

Procrastination and fear of failure — yes, they've been pretty much constant companions for as long as I can remember.

With the benefit of 20|20 hindsight, I can see now how both procrastinating and being fearful of failing have impeded my progress from childhood onwards — academically, in the corporate media world, and as a business owner. Exams not passed, promotions self-sabotaged, opportunities I've let slip out of my grasp.

They are still with me. The difference now is that I understand they're a product of my own thinking and as a result they've lost a great deal of their power. Not all their power — not yet — but they are significantly less disabling than they were.

I understand now that they are — as Damian says here and in his book *Do Nothing!* — inescapable, part of the human condition, and once you get your head around that, you're able to spend a lot less time beating yourself up when they cross your path. You can stand back, take a deep breath, and wait for the thought and the accompanying emotions to subside to the point where you can get past the obstacle you've put in your own way.

For sure, this doesn't always work first time and knowing how the process works doesn't guarantee you can instantly quell that internal dialogue: the one that might go: *"You should be doing that, not this"*... *"Yes, but looking for this on Amazon is so much easier and so much more instantly gratifying than calling that prospect"*... *"This is taking you down a time-hoovering and unproductive rabbit hole, but as soon as I've checked this out I really will get back to what I should be doing"*...

I still have these moments, but far fewer of them, and once I do feel an 'Amazon moment' — as it were — coming on, I stop, walk away from the screen and just let the thought loosen its grip and float out of my consciousness. Visualising thoughts as fluffy clouds in a blue sky may not work for everyone, but it works for me!

Also a part of my toolkit now is regular meditation — or mindfulness practice — at the start of the day. It really amplifies the whole process because it's taught me how to step right back from all my thoughts and emotions and just 'be' for 10 or 20 minutes at a time. I always emerge feeling re-energised, with heightened confidence and greater clarity.

And I also follow my intuition 100%. If it feels right, it is right. If it feels wrong, it is unerringly wrong. Your intuition, your innate ability to filter out what is and isn't good for you, really is your best friend and you override it at your peril. I've only gone against my gut instinct twice in business — and obviously not recently! — and on both occasions I ended up with significant bad debts, despite travelling the County Court Judgement route.

How does all this benefit my business? On a practical level, my time is spent much more productively, and at a strategic level I am more assured of my ability to make sound and sometimes bold decisions because I fully recognise that the only thing that can stop me staying headed in the right direction is my own unhelpful thinking.

For my clients, this means that they're now getting a far superior version of me — more confident, more decisive, more focused, and better able to serve them at a really high level.

www.eugenieverney.com

"Leave your front door and your back door open. Allow your thoughts to come and go. Just don't serve them tea." - Shunryu Suzuki.

ELEMENT FOUR: LAUNCH: WHY YOU DON'T EVEN NEED A BUSINESS TO BE IN BUSINESS AND HOW TO GET CUSTOMERS FAST!

"You must live in the present, launch yourself on every wave, find your eternity in each moment."
- Henry David Thoreau

OK, so you've got your 'why' - the driving force behind your actions. You've got some clarity on your goals and where you're headed, and you've been introduced to a new paradigm in thinking about fear and failure, making better decisions, and approaching entrepreneurial success from a very different perspective. Now what you need is something to work with, something really tangible - an actual business.

Alright, you might already have a business, I get that. But if you don't have one yet, here's the really good news: you don't even need one to start your entrepreneurial journey!

I discussed earlier in the book how you can get

a business up and running using websites such as Alibaba or JVZoo, Upwork and PeoplePerHour, but in terms of amplifying your expertise and making a positive change and impact on the world, you really don't need much more to get the ball rolling than a strategy. I've seen products and businesses starting up with nothing more than a squeeze page offering a new service or a pre-release of a book, asking for the money up-front. Their 'funnel' then goes into information capture mode, asking what you'd like to actually see in the product (or even the book). This is a really simple way to find out what your customers really want from your offering before you even get to sell it to them. Not a bad way to get the ideas from the end user with enough cash in the bank to finance the entire operation from pre start-up to launch.

Of course there are some of you who wouldn't want to take any money up front, I get that too. But then wouldn't you take money up front from a publisher who paid you to write a book about your expertise? So what's the difference? Someone is still asking you to deliver the goods in the future for something that doesn't exist yet. And you'd be happy to do it for them, so why not for a willing customer?

We'll talk a little more about books later, as this is one of the most effective ways to amplify your expertise and your brand to a larger audience. What's more, anyone in the world can do it... even with a simple pen and paper. But for now, let's concentrate on your passionate idea and how you can accelerate this into super success.

It's never been easier to launch a product or service than it is today. It's faster to find and communicate with your customers and the cost is lower than ever before, as globally connected, hyper-targeted social media speeds up the whole process. You can now sell your products directly to your customers and no one else has to be involved. You can get rapidly fast, if not instantaneous feedback on how your product or service is performing and obtain the tweaks necessary to turn it into a best-seller. Although there are numerous ways to launch a product, here are the primary launch path paths:

A 'Quick Launch' is where you already have a list of prospects or current clients. We'll discuss how to build the right type of list shortly. A 'Seed Launch' has been outlined already by taking an idea and getting your customers to give you the content (and a demand).

'Joint Venture Launches' piggy-back the sign up list of a relevant product or service business that compliments your own, without detracting from the overall value given by offering both, instead of individually. An example would be a crèche service joining forces with a wedding photographer. Both can form part of a service for a niche market, whilst strengthening their own value. 'Sequential or Evergreen Launches' cover the entire spectrum from: not launching at all, to continuously improving your product or service and offering it as a new idea each time... think carpet sales. 'Shadow Launches' use other people's products (or white label products as we discussed earlier) and you don't even need stock to make this into a business, as this can be done digitally.

OK, so that's the various types of launches covered... perhaps you've got a massive 'why' and some clear goals, but no idea about a product or service to offer as yet. If that's the case, start by thinking how you could connect your talent to an offering of some sort. What valuable information do you know that someone else doesn't? What have you succeeded at which can be turned into a 'lesson' or others to learn from? Find out who is making money or having an impact already in this area and see how you could do it better.

Then think of your route to market. Assuming you have a customer base who might be interested in your product, think of the products you buy and why you buy them, and use a particular type of market research that is very effective and much under-utilised called... talking to people! Sir Richard Branson even does it (see the Pricing chapter), so talk to your customers and find out from these conversations: what your audience is looking for; what problems they have and what opportunities they want to take advantage of. Understand how your audience consumes marketing and which marketing routes might work to attract more of them. To do this, you'll need to also understand where your audience hangs out online, what publications and blogs they read and who do they already listen to and trust.

It's crucial here to differentiate between your target customers and just any customers in general. Depending on the product or service you provide, everyone in the world might be a potential customer, especially if you supply food or funerals! But as we've already established in the previous chapters, if you focus on the entire market place, you are wasting valuable resources. To escape mediocrity faster, it's better to niche in a specific sector that will make it easier for you to find your customers and for your customers to find you. We have an accountant within the Circle who specialises in performance artists. She is forever being referred by her clients to other performers, because as a performer herself, she knows the industry well and can tailor her service to fit her customers wants and needs. The products and services she provides are not that much different to those offered to non-performers, but when she uses the language of her target market, they respond accordingly.

For larger organisations, a similar approach would be to segment their customer base. I've worked with one company that had fifteen very specific customer avatars. An avatar is a generalised description of someone, representing their attitudes, beliefs and behaviours. The great thing about these is they can be entirely made up and then tested for accuracy. I once worked with a client in the USA who wanted to launch an £18k well being product in the UK. I advised him to come up with an avatar of the type of person who would be prepared to buy this expensive ticket item. Expecting just a few paragraphs as a description, I was delighted when we next met and he'd created a three page 'dossier' on his target customer. She was 42 years old, had long dark hair and green eyes, went to the gym three times a week, had a husband who worked within finance in the City, had two children, both in private education... the description went on and in some depth. It even had some small details in, such as the type of car her husband drove (a black Audi A4). This entire description had been created by nothing more than his own imagination of who he 'thought' could afford his product. But what he did next was even more remarkable. He put a condensed version of this description out onto social media and asked his connections to 'find this lady'!

Within days, he had numerous responses saying how much the description reminded them of a person they already knew. He managed to narrow the search down until he found some very accurate matches and began even more in-depth market research. One lady in particular matched the description so well that it could have been her, albeit with dyed hair. Her husband even drove the same car in the description!

With some tweaks made to his marketing and even the product itself, he ended up joining a gym in the commuter belt when he moved to the UK and ran a workshop within three months, inviting just under 40 of his target 'avatars' to the event. Eighteen women in the room signed up for an £18k programme before the day had ended. Not a bad conversion rate for such a high priced ticket item!

The point is that he didn't even have a customer to start with and created one from his own imagination. I'm sure you have customers in your business that you'd love to clone more of. If only you could have another thousand 'Michelles' or 'Roberts'. They just seem to 'get' what you are all about and why you do what you do.

And then of course, they'll be the customers who are a total pain in the backside. You'll be wanting to get rid of them completely at the earliest possible opportunity, perhaps by handing them your competitor's business card!

There's something called the 80/20 rule or the Pareto Principle, which applies beautifully here. Vilfredo Pareto was an Italian economist who realised that 80% of the land in Italy was owned by 20% of the population. He went on to test his hypothesis in other areas in life and found it to be everywhere. 80% of the peas in his garden came from 20% of the pods. 80% of the sales in the local marketplaces came from 20% of the vendors. 80% of your own profits will come from 20% of your customers. 20% of the roads hold 80% of the traffic, and of that 20%, another 20% (so 4%) will contain another 80% of the traffic. Just look at the M25! It applies in any area where inputs drive outputs. So 80% of any clinical and problematic issues on any given day in a hospital will arise from 20% of the patients.

This is really handy to know when you start looking at the numbers in your business. It will also come in useful when we look at the chapter on time management and productivity, because you don't need to do everything, you only need to do the things that get you the best results!

So the success of any product launch lies in the traffic generation strategy before the launch and the amount of 'right prospects' who are genuinely interested in buying what you offer. We'll spend more time on this later on, but in the meantime, the first customer generation strategy we'll focus on is called

'Search Engine Optimisation' (SEO) but it's by far the slowest one. If your potential customers search for information on what you offer, you'll need to know and understand your audience and what they're looking for and the search terms they use to find what you offer before you consider SEO. Two excellent research tools to help you with this are the Google AdWords Keyword Tool and SEMRush.com. If you have an audience that is low on awareness of your name, they aren't going to search you out, so you need to go out to where they are and get them to come back to your website if you want them to be aware of you. This is where having a product or service that is searched for in enough volume to make your business worthwhile, but not having too much competition, really helps. To get a higher search placing in Google, there are many different factors that Google considers in trying to give the best possible service to their own customers. Is your website relevant and is it worthwhile? Do you have good quality information on there and do you provide the best possible service to Google's customers? To go into all of the details of what these factors are would take too much time, and they are constantly changing anyway, but if you're considering putting all of your eggs in the Google search engine basket, this might be a bad idea because you never know how and when Google might change their algorithms and cause your site to be ranked lower or even make it impossible to find... even if you aren't doing anything 'black hat' (which is a term given to SEO strategists who try to fool Google).

We had one EC member who had this issue with his online betting site. One day he was raking in the cash and the next day he didn't even have a business. He changed his site to cope with a number of different search algorithms and one of his new inventions started performing better than the previous search options, and this time he wasn't reliant on a single route to his site.

Speaking of Google, one of the best ways to drive traffic to your website is by using Google Adwords. This is the advertising model that Google uses to make its money. By placing adverts in the search engine above the organic search and to the side of the main page, you are effectively advertising your products and services right at the front of the shop window at precisely the time that your customers have decided to buy what you offer. But it's not cheap if you are in a saturated marketplace and it's even harder to get right.

At the EC, we have a team of Adwords specialists and are considered by Google to be one of the top 50 Global Adwords Agencies. We often see members who've been promised the earth by an adwords specialist only to discover that they've set up the account wrong, not included negative keywords or they are sending a large volume of traffic to the wrong type of website. Adwords success is part art and part science and to get Google Adwords working properly for you, I suggest you get advice before committing to it. The wonderful part of Adwords is that when it is working properly (when return exceeds costs) it's like turning on a tap of customers at will because you are in the right place at the right time... which is when they are ready to buy.

The next way to attract customers is by creating compelling content that search engines like and that your market loves and shares. This approach is called 'content marketing'. However, contrary to popular belief, you don't just create content to attract people to your site... you create it to engage with people, to get them to stick around, to know, like and trust you and eventually to convince them to sign-up and buy something from you. The more awareness your potential customers have about your product or service, the less you have to do to 'convince them' and the more actively they'll seek you out when they're ready to buy.

Unless your target market is living in the dark ages, they should be on email and you should therefore be building an email list right now. This is a traffic source that you can build organically right now. You need to think about your email list like a 'bank account' that you can reach into and pull traffic (and cash) from, on demand. I had to do this with a large tax bill once - and it worked. Simply by cultivating my list and giving them good value, then keeping them engaged - when I had to make a quick sale, I simply made a great offer and got the money in the bank quickly. Within hours in fact. Having an email list is such a simple thing to do and so often ignored by budding entrepreneurs, so ignore it at your peril!

To get people to sign up to your list, think of offering something that might attract your target customers and get you on their radar. An app for Android or iPhone can be bought 'off the shelf' nowadays and given away in return for contact details. A value packed e-Book could be written in a weekend.

You could record a video training series or create a useful template. The point here is to make something relevant and valuable for your target audience that goes to show who you are and the value you offer, and is available in exchange for their contact details. That's where their journey begins with you.

Video marketing is an area which simply has to be considered in the age of 4G, and the soon to be released 5G. It's never been easier to create superb looking video with the high quality lenses on our smart phones. Create a video solution for a problem, which is being searched for online on one of the two biggest search engines - that's Google and YouTube for those who don't know. If you don't have any content ideas, do a video overview for every blog post you've written or are going to write. The important thing to remember here is that it needs to be 'found' online, so putting the right keywords into the description and the correct tags, is essential. Look up Derrel Eves on Google to find some really superb videos on how to tag properly. Also put your own URL as the first part of the description to drive them to your sign up page. You can use other video platforms for hosting quality video, like Vimeo or Wistia, but YouTube is the second biggest search engine and the point of this exercise is for you to find customers, by your customers finding you first.

Have you ever listened to an interesting webinar? These are being done to death right now, but finding a webinar or podcast with quality content, which doesn't try and sell to you straight away is becoming harder and harder, which means there's an opportunity for you to stand out and show what an expert you are, and get people into your funnel by giving great value and starting to engage with them without selling first. If you have a 'live only' event, that people will work their schedule around to attend, it might be better than having recorded versions, as people tend to sign up for webinars and just listen to the recording. But with the best intentions, we all get busy and forget, which is exactly what's happening with the majority of webinars being hosted today. By offering a live only version with incredible content, your interested listeners will have to be there to receive it, so you'll be making more of an impact. Yes, you might lose individuals who simply couldn't make the broadcast, but you must stop thinking that everyone is your customer. You could also get an industry professional to do a webinar with you. They'll market the webinar to their list, which is another validation of their (and your) expertise, whilst you market the professional to your list. Then you each get a larger portion of participants who you can send to your own websites for email sign-ups. Blab.im is a live webinar platform which is currently very popular and very simple to use.

Consider writing guest blog posts and articles. When you write articles in publications or on blogs that your audience reads, you'll be directly in front of your target market as the expert. It takes good writing and kudos to get published though, so make sure the quality of your words is up to scratch and the research is sound. Also think about some adjacent products that your customers already use, and then write for the publications that promote these. Alternatively, get other experts to guest blog for you.

If your guest has a decent sized audience, you've just tapped into it. Going down the industry expert interviews route is a quick and easy win, as they instantly bring credibility and a built-in target market. Conversely, make someone from your team available to be interviewed as an industry expert at all times and make use of regional media to build a profile as the 'local expert', who are always on the lookout for content - so don't be shy to use your local status to get a foot in the door and access the ears of nearby customers.

You can also promote your guest blogs to a willing and able audience by infiltrating online communities such as Forums and LinkedIn Groups. Get to know the moderator or owner of the group first so they'll help promote your message. Alternatively, you could create your own online community. Find people in your industry on LinkedIn, see what groups they belong to, join these, then create yours and promote it to the other members of the group you're already in. Speaking of LinkedIn, make sure that your profile summary and title include the niched product or service you provide. We had one member come to our LinkedIn training course and by lunchtime he had a £25,000 order based on the changes he made to his profile in the morning session (see the full story in Element Seven). A customer who already knew him was looking for something in particular and didn't realize, until he updated his LinkedIn profile, that his company offered it.

Live speaking engagements give you credibility

and a built-in target audience that you can leverage to send traffic to your site. As you wrap up your speech, mention you had three other points you wanted to cover but didn't quite have the time, so instead they can go to mysite.com/conferencename to download the slides and the additional content instead. By sponsoring these conferences - you will often get the emails of participants prior to the event itself and when you attend them, treat it like another marketing opportunity... there's no reason you couldn't boost traffic from being around many other like-minded, industry types.

We'll discuss using social media later on as part of your amplification package, but bear in mind that anything you do can be put into a visual form, such as the processes you go through to make the positive change for your customers. These can then be made into an infographic and shared on sites like Pinterest and Instagram, which are proving incredibly powerful for many of our members. If you already have a visual component to your product, integrating with Pinterest and Instagram could drive huge amounts of traffic, but your images need to be good quality and tagged properly so people can find them. Don't forget, most of the big name websites such as LinkedIn, Pinterest and even Amazon, are actually search engines. We'll go into more detail on Amazon in the chapter on writing a book, later on.

If you want to be really savvy, use ad or banner retargeting, which serves adverts to those that have already interacted with you at some stage. This is a way of cutting down your marketing costs considerably, as you know they have already expressed an interest in what you do and you're only following that particular person and not marketing to everyone else. You might notice that after going to a specific website, you seem to see that product's adverts on every page you visit afterwards. This is retargeting in action. If you share a computer with your loved ones, it's also a really bad way to let them see what you're buying as a gift for Christmas... so be warned!

It's worth pointing out here that it takes an average of seven points of contact for your customers to notice your brand. That's seven times they see your logo or advert before it even consciously registers. This is actually good news, because most business owners give up trying to get your attention after showing you their product or service just once. They try something, think it doesn't work and give up completely. Just knowing this is going to serve you well, because persistence is the key... to just about everything in life.

Use offline direct mail to drive potential customers online. There is one inbox that is definitely under-utilised at the moment and that's the letterbox in your front door. Standing head and shoulders above the pizza delivery menus and taxi cards would be a coloured envelope with a hand written address on it. Wouldn't you be inquisitive enough to open that? What about putting a folded note inside telling you to go to a specific web address to find the answer to a specific question such as 'What makes you special?' or whatever question you put, which might inspire an action.

Referrals can really be the backbone of your business, especially if your product or service is something that is talked about in everyday conversations - cleaning companies and accountants being two very good examples. Very few businesses actually have a system in place for getting consistent referrals, so don't make that mistake. In essence, you are leveraging the audience and customer base you already have who already know, like and trust you and we all like to be able to pass on quality information and tips to our friends and family. If you've done a good job for someone, they'll want to tell others about it. It's human nature and yet many business owners fail to see the potential here to get more, good quality customers without too much effort. This is where the true power of testimonials and case studies really comes in. We all look for social proof when buying items online. Think of the last time you bought a book on Amazon for instance. If it had a few too many one star reviews, you might not even consider it. We look for social proof wherever we go, whether we know it or not. When we're out looking for a restaurant, we'll tend to pick the ones that look busiest, which is why the owners usually put the early arrivals by the window first.

Instead of shooting a straight forward video testimonials, do some fully featured case studies showing who the client is, what their pain was before you came along and how you made their dreams come true - kind of like the way that talent shows showcase the interesting artists. A short video showing this on your website is going to get so much more traction than a standard testimonial (or no testimonial at all).

Of course, using someone who already has credibility increases the power of this exercise, so if there is a leading industry figure or celebrity who might benefit from your product or service, try and get their endorsement. Some celebrities charge through the roof for this, but others don't and there's really no harm in asking. Then you can piggyback off their credibility, as often they'll promote it to their own audience, especially if it is done in a way that makes sense for them to do it.

You can also use this for effective public relations. Emma Blake, who runs PinStripe & Pearls found this out when Kate Middleton wore one of the dresses from their website. The designer of the dress hadn't planned for the large volumes of traffic to his own website and it simply couldn't handle the volume, so Emma's site became the intense focus of a global audience. By the time their phones had stopped ringing, they'd sold out of their entire website stock!

If you don't have any sort of an email list, there is still another method of email marketing. Although not as effective as creating your own segmented house list, buying email lists from places like Yell. com and Equifax can prove successful, as long as you are allowed to send unsolicited email and you do it in a way that is beneficial to the list. There are various types of email lists: Response Lists come from magazines, clubs, catalogues and warranty cards, but you'll need to check the hygiene of these first and sometimes the supplier will require a sample of whatever you are going to send out. Compiled Lists are gathered from public records, phone books, B2BProspector.co.uk or Experian, so beware of too many unsubscribes on these, which might affect your ability to send more emails, depending on your email provider. MailChimp are pretty hot on this, but you can always put your own unsubscribe button within the email which sends you an unsubscribe request, instead of it going to MailChimp directly. You control your own score this way, but you'll need to be on top of this, because if you continue to send emails once someone has unsubscribed, you could get in real trouble. One member got quite clever with this and had all the unsubscribes from his email list automatically send him an alert on his mobile. As soon as one came through, he would call the person up directly, saying he was the owner of the company and asked why they'd unsubscribed from his list. It was invariably because their inbox was out of control or the email they received wasn't relevant to their business, so he then asked them what would be relevant. This gave him valuable information as to what his customer was actually looking for and allowed him to tailor his products accordingly. As I keep highlighting, don't fall into the trap of thinking that everyone is your customer. If you try and please everyone, you'll end up pleasing no one.

Use press releases to alert local media of your uniqueness. They love to promote local businesses, and there's a good chance you might end up as a guest on one of their regular shows. Record the interview and send it to a larger station, taking out any 'Um's' or 'Er's' so you sound like a professional, and you might end up on the local BBC station. I used this technique and was being interviewed by Dr Phil on BBC Radio Bristol within two months. It works! Oh, and once you've done this, put 'As featured on the BBC' up on your website.

Try and get into the habit of creating a press release for everything... (even your blog posts) and sending them to a regular list of contacts. Every now and again, they'll take a bite, and you could end up in front of a much bigger audience in no time. My friend and mentor, Jamie Smart is an author, coach and speaker. He sent regular press releases to Sky News and was soon being interviewed on Sky Sports discussing sporting psychology when the England cricket captain, Andrew Strauss resigned. Again... it works!

People will tell you that press releases are dead... but if you are creative and consistent, you'll cut through the noise. These are just some of the links you may find useful for contacts:

http://www.prweb.com

http://www.businesswire.com

http://www.prunderground.com

http://www.marketwired.com

http://www.buzzstream.com

http://www.prnewswire.com

http://www.pitchengine.com

http://www.criticalmention.com

http://www.trendkite.com

http://www.mediamiser.com

http://www.smaudience.com

The next way to amplify your business and attract

the right type of customers is to win awards for the thing you're good at. Sign-up for, nominate yourself for, and otherwise try to win awards for anything and everything you can. Why? Because it is social proof on steroids. If you are an 'Award Winning' anything, it tells people that you went up against a whole bunch of your competitors and won, because some experts in the industry you are in, decided that you were better than them. We've had members who've told us that their unique selling proposition (category of one) is their customer service. "Fantastic" I tell them, "So all of your competitors go out of the way to be rude to their customers then...?" Of course not (although in one case this was actually true!). But to make this into something which will attract the right type of customers to your brand, there needs to be some sort of proof attached, and winning awards does just this. Even 'being nominated' will give you a credible reason to do a press release and get your name out there.

If you want to be really clever, find questions on Q&A sites like Quora or in the LinkedIn Groups and use that to write specific blog posts, create videos, or otherwise create rich-media content, which you can share back to the group. You already know it's relevant because someone's taken the time to ask about it. Have your PA, virtual assistant or staff member scour the Q&A sites for questions, then put these into a spreadsheet and create an editorial calendar. Be sure to note how many followers a question has on Quora (for instance) and answer them in the order of 'most followers' - going for maximum leverage first. Then 'answer' the question with a well-researched article, with a back-link to your content.

Sponsored content could be another route to get more leads, which is when you pay for an article on a website with really good traffic. Don't forget, your customers didn't start looking for a solution to their problem when you created your business, they are already some else's customers. If the sites where you do this have good reach and you do it right, it can be really worthwhile (think product reviews and advertorials). Many industry magazines will publish an article from you only if you also buy an ad in the publication - a little bit sleazy on their part perhaps, but effective nonetheless.

Set yourself up as a public speaker on membership sites or private paid communities where your target audience hangs out. I've seen a number of members do very well out of joining organisations such as Toastmasters International. It's a great way to prepare yourself for amplifying your brand. Get some speaking practice in by trying out local radio first and perhaps do a few hours' practice in front of the mirror too. I've done hundreds of paid speaking engagements now on the back of my book and it gets easier every time I do it (and more enjoyable). I've even done a TEDx talk about it!

You could also get traffic from the following ideas: T-shirts, Stickers, Meet-up Groups, Events, QR codes, Social Sharing widgets, Email signatures, Offline App-stores, Out of office notifications, Transactional email, Invoices/receipts, Commenting on blog posts, YouTube Ads, Integrations with other apps, Business cards, Distributors/intermediaries/trusted advisors, Snapchat, Newsletter ads, Twitter and Facebook Ads... in fact, the list is almost endless and is being added to all the time. When people complain about not being able to find customers, I always struggle to understand why. There are so many ways to attract the attention of the right types of customers if only you put your mind to work and think of some. It's then a case of getting on and just doing it. A really good example being... pick up the phone! I had a member who told me once that most of his business came from calling people, but he hated doing it. One quick mental flick of a switch later and he was on the phone making calls. In the two weeks that followed, he pulled in more business than the entire rest of the year combined. We often hate calling people simply because we don't like to be bothered by calls ourselves, so we think it's going to annoy them (and as we like to be loved), we don't do it. If this is you, re-read the fear chapter again and harness those thoughts!

CASE STUDY: SIAN NISBETT, DIZZY DUCKS NURSERIES

Getting customers is easy - you just need to know where to find them and once you find out where they 'hang out', it's easy to target them. For us, places like coffee shops, baby groups, doctors' surgeries, weighing mornings, NCT groups and the local park are ideal to find mums with young babies. We catch the attention of the children first by having branded balloons and then give leaflets to the parents. Even just having posters and leaflets available in these places increases enquiries.

Facebook also works brilliantly for us. That's because our target market, mums aged 25-45, hangs out there lots. Targeted Facebook adverts have become an easy, cost effective way of getting our message out to the masses. We use lead baits that will entice mums, whatever stage they are at in their parenting journey. For example, for a pregnant mum we have 'Back to work guides', 'What you need to know about looking for childcare' and 'Top tips for searching for your perfect nursery'. For new mums we have slightly different lead baits such as 'Cutting the cost of childcare' and various 'How to…'

leaflets on issues such as teething and nappy rash. In addition, our 'When should I search for my perfect nursery?' blog post is very popular.

For mums of slightly older children, we target them with our 'School readiness: How preschool brings out the best in your child' booklet. We have hard copies of all our lead baits and use them where appropriate.

Our website has 10 ways of leaving your information at any one time. This includes signing up for the lead bait material, enquiry forms, call back forms and even a live chat facility. The enquiries go directly into our database where they are systematically followed up using our sophisticated Customer Relationship Management (CRM) system. This includes calls, direct mail and emails encouraging the parent to book a nursery visit.

Once a parent has visited, the contact schedule drops into the next sequence, encouraging registration. This also involves calls, direct mail and emails. Once someone enquires with us, they remain in our marketing funnel receiving a minimum of one email per week until they either unsubscribe or join us.

Open days are also a great way of getting customers. We have certain elements that we incorporate into every event. Firstly, we always have a well-known 'character' attend. Our best performers are Peppa Pig or Ben & Holly. These appeal to both sexes, and parents are much more inclined to come along to an open day if their child can get their photo taken with a TV favourite.

We open our days up to everyone, using targeted Facebook adverts to encourage people to sign up. Usually the 'pull' of a meet and greet with the character is enough. We ask people to book free tickets through our CRM, which are delivered to them prior to the event. This has a number of distinct advantages:

1. We know how many people are coming to the event
2. We have 'booking slots' so we can stagger the flow of people throughout the day
3. We get the families' contact details (name, email)
4. We also get their physical address (to send the tickets out to)

This information is collected on the booking page

which then goes to a thank you page asking one further question: 'When will you require childcare?' Immediately, within 6 months, 6-12 months, 12 months +, or never. This flags any hot leads that we need to concentrate on during the open day. You will always get people who come along with absolutely no intention to sign up and you don't want to be wasting all your time with them.

We then run a competition for attendees to post their character meet and greet pics, which gets our social media channels buzzing.

The customer journey is carefully mapped out: from the first contact point, through to the day they leave us to go to school and we look to add value at every step. This means that parents often recommend us to their friends and the same cycle begins again. Without doubt, word of mouth advertising is our biggest way of recruiting new families.

Dizzy Ducks Day Nurseries consists of five nurseries, two out of school clubs, three holiday clubs and employs 150 staff. Call Dizzy Ducks on 01268 545904 or visit www.dizzyducks.co.uk

ELEMENT FIVE: NUMBER CRUNCHING: THE AWESOME POWER OF PRICING RIGHT, MEASUREMENT AND HOW TO SCALE UP

"Price is what you pay. Value is what you get."

- Warren Buffett

In this chapter we are going to look at pricing strategies, measuring the crucial numbers in your business and the scalability (or otherwise) of your business model. We are also going to look at the most common mistakes business owners make when they start and why 96% of businesses are doing it wrong.

In the Pricing Strategy course we run at the National Support Centre in Birmingham, the first question I ask attendees in the room is how many of them have raised their prices in the last five years, three years or one year. Invariably a number of hands shoot up and then we go around the room and ask how the price increase affected their sales? In nearly every single example they didn't have any problems at all as a result of putting their prices up. In fact, they invariably attracted *more* customers as a result.

You'll need to start thinking about your pricing in a slightly different way as we go through this chapter, because too many business owners focus on the entire marketplace as their customers. They are focused on what the *majority* will pay, rather than finding the small group of people who really *value* what they offer. I will show you in this chapter how your pricing choices will define your prosperity, because as the saying goes *"You can go to the ocean with a teaspoon or a bucket, the ocean doesn't care."*

Another activity that I run at the training courses is when I ask attendees what compelled them to make their last three expensive purchases - what were the underlying drivers in their decision to buy? This often proves interesting as well, because when we go around the room again and start to get a real indication of how and what we all value, it starts to become apparent what true value actually means to each of us.

Then I like to show examples of Entrepreneurs Circle members who have put their prices up and what's occurred as a result. For instance, Mark Hammond, who runs a marquee hire business said:

"Thanks to the Entrepreneurs Circle for telling me to increase my prices and give a higher level of service and showing me that customers won't buy just on price alone." This is all about how you can put your prices up, give added value, and sell more to the <u>right</u> customers as a result.

The first common pricing mistake made by business owners is when they set prices to 'industry norms and/or competitor's pricing'. If you are following industry norms, you have no real clue about what your ideal customers truly value. This is understandable because as start-up businesses, we tend to look at the competition and what they're charging and try to undercut them to gain any sort of a foothold in the marketplace. However, if another start-up using the same business model comes in to undercut you, and your customers decide to jump ship (because they are not loyal and only after the cheapest price), your profit margins will have shrunk to zero or worse. This is an unsustainable business model - just look at the budget airline business. Put simply, if you are attracting bargain hunters or cheapskates, you are simply fishing in the wrong pond. Your customers should be the ones who 'get' what you do, 'why' you are of value to them and be loyal customers who will not jump ship at the slightest sign of a discount from elsewhere. This leads to the next often made assumption about what your customers will and will not pay for a high quality service. Unless *you* are your customer, and by this I mean that you have created your product or service specifically for yourself to fill a gap in the market, and unless you talk to your customers or potential customers on a regular basis, you will not have any idea what they truly value and what they may be willing to pay for it.

I once employed a cleaning company who came to our house on a cold call and asked me what I required as part of a valued cleaning service. They said that a bespoke service usually appealed to their best and most valued customers, which of course, appealed straight away to my ego! They then asked me what would I like to have 'from the cleaning menu' to make my experience 100%. This included added extras such as oven cleaning, limescale removal and even a 'wardrobe refresh'. During the conversation, I also told them what had bothered me most about all of our previous cleaners and they made extensive notes and promised to make my ideal cleaning requirements a reality. It wasn't cheap by any means, but I didn't care. It was what I wanted, so I was willing to pay for it, and all from a cold call. They arranged for a clean that very day just to prove their quality, and it was incredible. I didn't wake up that morning thinking about cleaners, but I went to bed that night, not only thinking about my new cleaners and my nice clean house, but also about what an amazing job they'd done in selling and delivering a high quality premium product by just ringing my doorbell. A very simple example of why talking to your customers and potential customers to find out what they truly value is so important. Sir Richard Branson still flies regularly on his airline to speak to his customers first hand and see how their experience matches up to his (and their own) expectations. If speaking to customers is an essential part of Sir Richard's business strategy, don't you think it should be part of yours?

The fact is, pricing assumptions exist in your own head. Just because you think someone will not pay for an exclusive offering, doesn't make it true, *until* you test it out. We've had so many examples of this in the EC, of crazy, hair-brained ideas with a price tag to match, that have been snapped up, simply because they were available. But the greatest thing about having exclusive and premier offerings in your business is that it raises the *perceived* value of all of your other products and services. This is actually how expensive handbags get sold. By putting the expensive item next to a *really* expensive one, the 'cheaper' bag looks better value. This is called decoy pricing and is a pricing technique that a lot of our members now use to sell more items at better profit margins.

Another pricing fail in a similar vein is 'commoditised thinking'. You'd think for example, that window cleaning or a car wash is a commodity. After all, it's just a bucket of water and a sponge... isn't it? Not when you have a non-commodity mindset. Just ask Martin O'Connell, the EC member who has an exclusive window cleaning service for celebrities. It's not cheap and it comes with all sorts of upmarket offerings, like recycled spring water (Madonna insists on this apparently), but he's made it into a non-commoditised, successful business. He's recently been asked to clean the windows of the Google head quarters and the most expensive house in the UK, owned by the Saudi Royal family and cashing in at a whopping £280 million (the house, not the job)!

Or what about an £8,000 car wash... only available if you own a super or vintage car? This particular business owner has an exclusive list of clients including city bankers, footballers and celebrities. It takes three weeks to complete the clean and includes stripping the entire car and laser cleaning the paintwork. His 'category of one' is to promise a 'Better than showroom finish.' This won't be for your average happy shopper in the ASDA car park, but then they're really not his target market.

You see, if you try and market your product or service to everyone who might want what you have, you're wasting good marketing money. You want to attract the minority and repel the majority by offering something exclusive and valuable to those affluent enough to truly value it. And the most valued customers will value their *own time* above all else, so if they need something doing properly, they would rather pay once and trust it gets done, than scrimp and save a few pounds only to have to ask for it to be done again. That's poor use of their own time.

It's usually at this point in a training session or a one-to-one that I might have to do a bit of mental tweaking with the business owner who doesn't feel *worthy* enough offering exclusive products or services. It's quite simple when it comes down to it. Do you want to make your business a success, or struggle to get by financially? Usually it's the former. In which case, why would you want to be selfish and keep your superior talents hidden from those that will appreciate them most?

Another thing to realise is that by charging more for your products and services, you will be able to provide a *better* product or service for your customers. If you think you're saving them money, you've got the wrong pricing mindset.

It's worth also pointing out here, that a very important part of your business... is your numbers. By this I mean knowing what is happening in your business using accurate measurements.

How many customers do you have?

Where have they come from?

What made them come to you?

How much did it cost to turn them into a customer (including factoring in your own time)?

Who comes to your website and where do they come from?

How long do they stay and why do they leave?

What is your average customer lifetime spend?

What parts of the business are the most profitable and why?

How many debtor days do you have?

Which parts of your business can you assign costs to?

Where is your business headed in terms of projected numbers?

How much have you assigned to your marketing?

What *can* you assign to marketing spend?

How much of your staff time is actually billable to your clients?

How much are each of your staff adding to the bottom line (it should be three times their salary in productivity)?

These are just some examples to get you started...

"In God we trust... all others bring data."
- William Edwards Deming

We're not just talking about a basic Profit and Loss account here, we're talking in depth numbers so you know what your business is actually doing and what you can do about it if it's not performing as well as it should be.

In this regard, we talk a great deal within the EC about having a 'pro-active' accountant, not an historical one. Historical accountants take your year-end accounts, do some crunching and tell you if you still have a business or not. Pro-active accountants will go through your business plans with you and work out a way for you to make them into reality. They then keep you informed of your progress and suggest alterations to get you to your target faster and more efficiently. Now that's a useful accountant! We have numerous award winning accountants within the EC who will do this for you and who are helping our members already take their businesses to super success.

With regard to this last point, how do you know if and when your business is ready to go to the next level? Scaling a business *can* be a very risky thing to do. If you try to grow anything and there are cracks in the foundations, these cracks will grow larger as you expand, exposing all sorts of problems. At least if you have a really good hold on the numbers within your business and are getting regular, professional advice from those who've had experience in this area, you will stand a better chance of making better choices.

If you are considering taking your business to the next level and your goals include rapid expansion, then the next chapter on staff is an essential read for you. Growing too fast, sometimes called 'growing broke' can kill a business, even if you are doing all of the basics right. Having the right advice throughout this process and being all over your numbers to a point of obsession is definitely the best strategy. You can't be too careful when it comes to growth, because of the cracks/foundations analogy already highlighted. As soon as you begin to expand, if there are any small issues within your business, these will get bigger and bigger and can ultimately lead to total instability. The Entrepreneurs Circle runs a number of courses and Mastermind groups for ambitious business owners who want to take this next step. They are facilitated by trainers who've been responsible for growing successful multi-national organisations, so they know what they're doing.

Our aim within the EC is to help business owners escape mediocrity and the fastest way to do this is to position yourself as an expert in a niche which is valued highly. Like the HR company which specialises in HR for golf clubs. A high value ticket item for high net worth customers. Or the accountant who specialises in 'ethical businesses', the electrician who only deals in smart home technology or the painter and decorator who specialises in custom finishes and only deals with specific, award winning interior designers. It's your business, so you get to choose whom you work with, and by specialising in a niche sector or market, you get to work with specific individuals who can find you more easily as the expert within that field. It's also easier for you to remain as a thought leader in a narrow field instead of trying to keep ahead in broader markets.

One question I get asked a lot is when to use 'free' as a lure to potential new customers. As a rule of thumb, people don't value 'free'. If you have a free coaching session, a free consultation, or a free report, it's unlikely it will be treated with as much attention or respect as one that costs something. John Staves from Michael Aubrey Partnership is an EC member who works in the construction sector. He used to offer free consultations and his time was fully booked and spent with roughly two thirds time wasters and a third interested parties. Against the advice of his colleagues and the 'industry norm', he started charging for consultations. His diary cleared by two thirds, but the conversions of the remaining third actually increased! In other words, he had filtered out the time wasters, and increased the perceived value of his service. So he then put his prices up and as a result, got more enquiries, plus the value of the work coming in also increased. Michael Aubrey has just expanded (again) and recently opened their new offices in Wokingham.

However, 'free' *can* still be used tactically to increase profits. There is a website in the US called KidsBowlFree.com, which lists bowling alleys where, you guessed it... kids can bowl... for free. The reason this works is because the business owners know their numbers. They realise that by bringing in kids for free, they are actually bringing in increased profits, because for every three kids who come to bowl, there's an adult with a credit card who also has to buy food, drinks, a game for themselves, shoe hire and a multitude of other upsells within the business.

Or what about the example of the Chinese takeaway that offered free wantons and a bottle of fizzy drink with orders over £30. Their average customer spend was £25, so by offering this 'freebie', it actually increased profits. What's more, they brought in additional patronage from competing takeaways with their offer and the average customer spend actually increased to over £33 as a result. Again, by having a proper understanding of your numbers within the business, you can start to create offers that attract the right type of customers without affecting your bottom line in a negative way.

Another example of using a 'loss leader' to increase profits would be the guitar maker who sold plectrums on eBay at a loss, but by doing so, he was collecting the data of his target market... guitar players. Not a bad way to increase his list at a small loss, which was of course - a marketing spend, just like placing an advert. Again, by adjusting his mindset and thinking differently, he was able to tap into a rich vein of willing customers with a clever marketing strategy.

There are other ways to attract higher value customers to your business by using some clever brain psychology. By introducing scarcity into your marketing, for instance, you are actually taping into a human inclination to place higher value on objects that are harder to obtain, and a lower value on those that are abundant. We want what we cannot have and this drives us to desire the object even more. What's more, social proof is a contributing factor because if a product is sold out, or stock is extremely low, we interpret this to mean it must be really good, since everyone else appears to be buying it.

Pricing affects our physiology too. Researchers at Stanford and the California Institute of Technology showed in a tasting experiment where volunteers who were told they were tasting an expensive wine and a cheap wine - they were exactly the same wine - not only did they describe the wine they thought was more expensive as better quality, but the part of the brain which experiences pleasure also became more active. *"What we document is that price is not just about inferences of quality, but it can actually affect real quality,"* said Baba Shiv, Sanwa Bank Limited, Professor of Marketing who co-authored the research paper that followed. *"So, in essence, [price] is changing people's experiences with a product and, therefore, the outcomes from consuming this product."*

What does this mean for you as a business owner? Well, in short, when you charge more for your products and services, your customers actually enjoy it more! That's right, charging less is actually <u>bad</u> for them - the more expensive it is, the better we *think* it is!

There's a whole bunch of other pricing strategies which we could cover here, like using unusual guarantees, upselling, price anchoring, memberships, auctions, target costing, yield and performance based pricing and more, but there's not enough room to go into these here. We cover these strategies along with many others in depth in the Pricing Strategy training courses at our National Support Center in Birmingham and our Southern training courses in Guildford. If you'd like to come on one of these days, then please contact the Entrepreneurs Circle on 0121 765 5551 to find out more.

To finish off this chapter, I just wanted to tell you how a study in the 1990s by the consulting firm McKinsey & Co of 2,463 companies showed how a simple 1% increase in your prices (assuming no loss of volume) will result in an 11% overall operating profit. It's no surprise therefore that large companies such as Starbucks regularly employ this strategy. And you thought that latte was just affecting your waistline!

We'll look at health and well being later on, so perhaps that latte will have to be shelved if you want super success. One last thing to mention on pricing, is to make sure that your customers are able to purchase from you easily. What do I mean by this? Well, if you are going to make a sale, then please make sure your customers are able to pay you either right there and then, or preferably before you deliver. As a business coach, I wouldn't dream of putting on a training event without payment upfront first. Why should your business be any different? What's more, if I charge thousands up front, I'll have a room full of eager participants ready to learn on day one. Don't just follow your industry norms, think about how you could do it differently and break the mold. Just look at Amazon Prime and how they've changed home shopping with charging premium prices for a super fast service.

CASE STUDY: STEVEN MARKHAM: CO-FOUNDER/CEO - VFLOORPLAN LTD I 'FROM BROWSER TO BOOKING'

I am co-founder and CEO of Cubicspace (in 1997) and together with Steve Baker, our CTO and Lead Programmer, we have co-founded vFloorplan. Cubicspace is a software developer of exciting award-winning 3D real-time tools, and patent-pending technologies, which enable the creation, movement and interaction within believable 3D representations of the physical world. vFloorplan's slogan is 'from browser to booking' and we are the developer and supplier of a popular and growing range of interactive 3D floorplans (vFloorplans), CGI visualisations, and online experiences for Hospitality, Travel, Real-Estate, Shopping and Medical.

Since 2013, vFloorplans have been sold to many prestigious clients within the hospitality sector and our innovative and original products continue to be tested at multiple price points.

We started with a non-interactive picture version of a hotel floorplan and sold it at a low launch price per floorplan to a prestigious UK hotel chain. Six months later we launched our first two interactive versions and increased the prices by 300% and 500% respectively. But each time, we also increased the value given to the client. We increased the prices initially by 75% and enabled earlier clients with older versions to buy upgrades. By December 2014 the products were at version

2 and prices increased by another 100%. A year later we launched version 3 and have successfully sold them to two new major clients at another 85% increase. These latest versions represent an overall increase in selling prices of 900% more than the first interactive version, but in each case our clients have had a significant double and triple digit return on their original investment.

Now we have added a new way to capture leads and generate sales that was not present in the original products. Customers can clearly see how many rooms within a venue are for hire, on which floors (helping navigation around the larger venues) and where they are located within the venue, plus the shape of the rooms and how the room looks laid out for different room styles like banquet, cabaret, classroom etc. Seeing the options of partitioned rooms, customers can consider breakouts and receptions, which increases their own customer's spend. We are generating significant benefits, which justify even higher prices for single venue clients and we are convinced we are still not yet at optimum pricing.

For clients with multiple locations, our new

continuity business model enables us to reduce the entry price of our latest version of vFloorplans (v3) by up to 90%, by adding a commission for bookings made through our vFloorplans using our new online booking and management system.

Our attention to detail and interactive approval process produces perfect projects, meets our client briefs and over delivers on their expectations. If you can deliver a high return on investment to your customer, then it really doesn't matter what your price is.

"vFloorplan makes it easy to navigate our venue, detailing the variety of options we have to offer clients, enabling them to see an overview of how our meeting rooms and boxes can be laid out for events. It's a brilliant addition to our website and client feedback has been very positive." - Carlo Zoccali | Meetings & Events Manager - Arsenal Football Club

"I was amazed and pleased at how functional and clear the renderings were - Wow! vFloorplan allows our guests to visualise the rooms and layouts in an easy to use and exciting format, while also presenting the location of the room within the facility.

I love it and am looking forward to adding some other exciting upgrades in the near future!" - Crista Tompson | Director of Sales & Marketing - SMG/ Century Center, USA.

Contact: steven@vfloorplan.com

www.vfloorplan.com / 01908 889294

Entrepreneur Success Formula

ELEMENT SIX: SYSTEMS: MAKING IT ALL WORK SMOOTHLY AND SOME TIME MANAGEMENT

"Inefficiency is easy to correct, if you can find the cause of it..." - Unknown

There are 1,440 minutes in every day no matter who you are and what you're doing. There are always the same amount of minutes in a day, from the one on which you were born, until the day you die - unless you decide to become an astronaut and start spending your days in orbit and messing around in black holes or discover the secret of immortality! For everyone else who says they don't have enough time, not having enough of something that is a constant is a total nonsense. There is time, and time is perpetual. What you don't have enough of... is focus.

If you focus your attention and energies in the right place and have the systems and processes in place to make these actions efficient and effective, you will not only have reclaimed your 'lost' time, but you will be halfway there on your journey to entrepreneurial success. Fortunately the time spent reading this chapter will prove to be very effective in changing your approach to systems and managing your time better.

We looked in the previous chapter at the Pareto Principle, or the 80/20 rule, and the same approach applies to time. You will spend roughly 80% of your time doing work that results in 20% of your results. And if you can find out what the remaining 80% consists of, you can either get someone else to do it (PeoplePerHour.co.uk is a great resource for this), or stop doing it altogether. You'll then be able to focus on the 20% of actions that will give you better results.

"The wisdom of life consists in the elimination of non-essentials." - Lin Yutang

So how do you know what is the most effective use of your time and what are the essential tasks? Well it starts with understanding your numbers, as we discussed in the previous chapter. Unless you actually know what is working and what isn't - by measuring it - you'll just be guessing. Having said that, you might already have an inkling that surfing Facebook for cats falling off sofas is not actually effective use of your time – your wisdom will guide you on this one!

To fully understand your measurements, you also need to have a clear goal and some sort of time schedule. This is why the previous chapters were so important, so if you brushed over these, I would suggest you go back and read them properly and do the exercises. Once you have clarity on your goals and why you are doing them, it then makes the next part so much easier, because then you can ask yourself the simple question: "Am I doing the most important thing right now?"

Doing only the tasks that are truly important and will help you get to where you want to go, is the key to effectively utilising your time. We are incredibly lucky in the Entrepreneurs Circle to have an Olympic medalist as one of our trainers at the National Support Centre. Ben Hunt-Davis won a gold medal in the rowing eights at the 2000 Sydney Games. The course he runs is called: 'Will it make the boat go faster?' and is based upon his book by the same title.

In 1998, Ben and the rest of the UK rowing eights team had just failed abysmally in the World Championships in Cologne. But Ben had a dream...

to win an Olympic gold medal. Fortunately, this was also the dream of the rest of the crew, so they made a decision there and then that they would win gold in Sydney in less than two years' time.

The problem was, there was a reason they'd done so badly at the World championships, and it seemed pretty insane to carry on doing their training in the same way. To cut a long story short, one that the book describes in brilliant detail I should add, they came up with a simple phrase that was instrumental in guiding their decisions over the grueling weeks and months of hard work that lay ahead. A simple phrase that would tell them if the behaviour they were considering was essential, effective and efficient.

You may already have guessed what the phrase is by now (as this is the title of his book) but let's have a think about how they applied it. When asked by a friend if he'd like to go for a drink at the local pub, he would apply the question. Of course, drinking alcohol would not make the boat go faster. Getting up early in the morning and going training in the cold, icy conditions... would this make the boat go faster? Yes, it would. What about being invited to a wedding by one of his best friends? That's missing some training and drinking again. Nope, it's not going to make the boat go faster. What about attending the opening ceremony for the Olympics, a once in a lifetime experience? Standing around for hours holding a flag is not going to make the boat go faster, so the team decided to watch from their hotel room instead. Can you see how it makes it so much easier to decide between two alternatives when there is absolute clarity on your vision and purpose?

Another way to eliminate alternatives is to ask yourself *"Which problem do I want to solve?"* We all have busy lives, but being busy is not a sign of productivity. In fact I would suggest it's the very opposite. It's a sign that the busy person hasn't thought about what is essential first, because ultimately, it's not about how to get more done, it's about how to get the right things done. By asking yourself which problem needs solving, you are suggesting that by overcoming this problem (first) it will remove obstacles for other things to happen. This is often the first place I will go to when coaching someone, as it's easy to miss the obvious when you're so close to it.

Let me give you an example. I was recently coaching someone who felt overwhelmed with the choices available to market their product. Before we went headfirst into a discussion about the benefits of spending time on Facebook advertising versus understanding Pinterest, I asked the question: *"Which problem do you actually want to solve here?"* My client got quiet for a moment as she reflected, and replied:

> *"Well I'm actually trying to get some more sales."*
>
> *"How many do you need?"* I responded.
>
> *"Three a month.""*
>
> *"Where do you currently convert prospects into paying customers?"*
>
> *"Face to face."*
>
> *"And how do these customers find you?"*
>
> *"Via searches on Google... we've previously been running a successful Google Adwords campaign."*

Silence...

> *"I should be doing more Adwords, shouldn't I...?"*
>
> *"Yup."*

The problem is, we live in a world where choice is everywhere, and it's so easy to get sucked into believing that we should be doing everything, just because we hear others are doing it. This is where having clarity on your goals really helps. It makes it so much easier to make effective choices with an end goal in mind, just like Ben and his team. We often make decisions in life harder than they need to be. It's as if we see the simplicity but decide it can't be that simple, so we make it harder and more complex than it needs to be. We've already discussed in the mindset chapter how to make better decisions and the power of knowing that there is no such thing as failure, only feedback and lessons learned. So go for the simplest option, the one that feels right.

"You cannot overestimate the unimportance of practically everything" - John Maxwell

I mentioned in the introduction how 'if you don't prioritise your life, someone else will' and 'everything you do in life is as a result of the choices you've made up until now'. Perhaps now might be the time to make the decision to 'stop doing stupid stuff', crack on and make your life not only what you want it to be, but what it should be. Yes, you could be watching reality TV instead of planning your life and finding clarity. Yes, you could choose to stay in bed and not write your book. Yes, you could make the easy choices time and time again for the rest of your life, but then you'd just be letting real life slip you by.

Think for a minute about everything in your life that you are proud of and how you managed to achieve it. I'll bet that it wasn't easy. It took determination and consistent effort. Passing exams... learning to walk, run and cycle... winning prizes or awards... creating something of real value... even parenting! Whatever it is, you should reflect for a moment on precisely what it took to become who you needed to become to make it a reality.

You see, we live in an edited world. Technology has given us the ability to be able to peer into the lives of others, but for the most part, these glimpses are mere highlights - the bits that we want people to see, rather than the real truth. Because of these edited highlights, it looks like there is a fast-track to success, so we're always on the lookout for the secret to how they achieved it so quickly. But therein lies the problem. They didn't. There is no quick fix. There is no magic formula or secret sauce. This book is as close as you're going to get to one, and you've got me repeating the same things over and over again: Your habits create your world. Get clarity on your purpose. Understand mindset and use it to your advantage. Implement, implement, implement... test, test, test.

None of this is rocket science or perhaps even anything you've not heard before, and I'm afraid that you're going to keep on hearing it again and again, so you might as well make a choice right now to start to do what is necessary to change your life and become successful. No one else is going to make the choice for you.

Starting right now, tell yourself: "I can't do everything, so I will only do the most important things. I can't always control the options that I'm faced with, but I can control my choices from those options from now on."

So if you're ready to continue, let's look at some processes that will help you to get the right things done more effectively and efficiently and let's start with the night before:

Botty rule 37:
"Today ain't over till tomorrow's planned."

I have a system, one that works very well for me and for my clients. It involves some highly sophisticated equipment called... a 'pen and paper'! It's very high tech, but takes only seconds to turn on and start using. Just before you go to bed at night, take out a notepad and write a list of everything you need to do the next day. I then use 'Eisenhower's Urgent/ Important Principle' (named after the President) to look at each task and ask the following question: Is this task important and urgent, important but not urgent, not important but urgent, not important and not urgent? Important activities have an outcome that leads to me achieving my goals (whether these are professional or personal), whilst urgent activities demand immediate attention and are usually associated with achieving someone else's goals. These are often the ones we concentrate on and demand our attention because the consequences of not dealing with them are immediate. This simple marking system then gives me my priorities for the next day on a 1-4 grading scale. It requires me to think through each task and make a decision based upon my desired outcomes. I then have a plan for the following day and can sleep easily.

"Give me six hours to chop down a tree and I will spend the first four sharpening the axe"
- Abraham Lincoln

If you've been near anyone who's a member of the Entrepreneurs Circle, you'll no doubt have heard a great deal about something called '90 Minutes'. This is the time put aside each day that we encourage our members to work 'on their business' and not 'in the business'. As an example, if you are an accountant, the time spent 'in' your business is when you are working on your client's accounts, and the time spent 'on' your business is spent on your marketing and promotion to get and keep more customers.

The concept of the 90 Minutes stems from a conversation that Nigel Botterill had when he first set up in business on his own. One of his business mentors, Martin Howey once asked: *"What's the most important thing you need to do to make your business successful?"* After taking a moment to think it through, Nige responded *"Getting and keeping customers,"* to which Martin replied *"I agree... so when are you getting and keeping customers today then, Nige?"*
Nigel's business life changed that day, because

he was always busy, coming into the office early, checking emails, dealing with phone calls, helping staff and working hard. However he wasn't dedicating any time to just getting and keeping customers. The very next day he started 90 minute sessions dedicated to doing just this and has been doing it every morning for the past twelve years. There's even a sign on his door, which comes into operation when he's doing his sessions saying: 'Do not disturb, unless the building is on fire!' It only took one staff reprimand for everyone to take him seriously and it's because of these 90 minute sessions working on his business that Nige has managed to create eight, million pound plus businesses in eight years. It's important to do these 90 minute sessions uninterrupted. Turn off all your emails and your phone and set this time aside to think carefully about how to get and keep more customers.

I often get asked what to 'do' in these 90 minute sessions and apart from the long list of ideas in the Launch chapter, just having time to sit and reflect is often under appreciated in business. As we've already mentioned, taking time away from looking at problems directly leads you to the solutions you require, especially if you've struggled to find an answer already. Having a space that is conducive to this is an essential part of the process. A cluttered office will simply not help you think straight.

Taking time out to think is so crucial to entrepreneurial success. Problem-solving thinking arrives when we stop looking directly at the problem, and having the ability to tap into our creativity is vital if we are to keep ahead of the game and innovate. Imagination is, after all, the prime source of every form of human achievement. Just think of the times when you've had your brightest ideas or your most game changing thoughts. My clients often tell me that it was when they were on holiday, away from the pressures of work and able to relax and let new, insightful thinking emerge. Taking time away from the business should therefore be treated as much a part of your business as being 'in work'.

There is now significant evidence to show the importance of play in creativity, imagination and well being. This also applies to your staff and how they get to be their most creative and at their best. If you look at the most innovative global companies, they value 'play in the workplace' highly. Play is fun and triggers the release of endorphins, the body's natural feel-good chemicals, which relieves stress and can even temporarily relieve pain. Play stimulates the mind and boosts creativity - it's been shown that young children learn best when they are playing and that applies to adults too. We learn new tasks more efficiently when they're fun and we're in a relaxed and playful mood. Play improves brain function and also stimulates the imagination, helping you adapt and problem solve.

The social interaction through play, laughter and fun, can also foster empathy, compassion, trust and intimacy with others, and developing a playful nature can help you make new friends and form better business relationships. In the words of George Bernard Shaw, "We don't stop playing because we grow old; we grow old because we stop playing."

But what if the unexpected happens? 'Stuff' happens everyday to knock us off-course. We get hijacked all the time by the unforeseen... so plan for it! Create buffers of time to be able to deal with unanticipated events so you can deal with them and still get back on course with what really matters. However, it's a good idea to underestimate the time it takes to get things done, so keep this in mind when deciding how long to allow.

Having the ability to say 'No' is also an essential skill. If someone comes along with their own agenda, it's up to you to head this off at the pass. Don't let 'time vampires' suck your diary dry whilst your entrepreneurial success and the lives of those who depend on you suffer as a result. I liken this to allowing a thief in your business. If someone was stealing from you and you found this out, you'd be hard pushed to give them a second chance. So why allow other people to steal your time? Be relentlessly unforgiving with anyone who thinks that your time is there to be hijacked. Firmly and clearly, tell them what you are doing, why it is important and that they will need to leave you to get on with your mission and purpose. With this in mind, you are only as strong as your weakest link, so if there are obstacles in the way (like time vampires), you'll need to think about how you can remove them. This is another example of 'clearing the clutter'.

If you're still struggling to work out what needs doing first, then ask yourself the following question: "If I could only choose one thing to do right now to make the gap between where I am now and where I want to be smaller, what would be the most effective action?" then focus on the task in hand and keep going until you break the back of it. The feeling you'll get when this happens is amazing. We spend so much time in our heads in the past and future, yet it is only in the here and now that anything actually gets done. Concentrated and inspired effort will therefore give you the momentum you need to make good progress.

Having a good routine will help you to be able to get into the right mindset and be more efficient and effective. We'll talk more about how you can catalyse the whole Entrepreneur Success Formula by adding in the secret sauce of health and well being later on... but for now, be aware that everything you do as an entrepreneur will affect your business. Everything you eat and drink, the amount of sleep you get and your physical health, are all part of your business going forward from here on in. And as such, a routine that incorporates all of these parts of the formula will help enormously. Hal Elrod has written a superb book called *'The Miracle Morning'* in which he suggests a routine starting early in the morning. This can include doing exercise to keep your mind and body healthy, doing your 90 Minutes working on your business and eating properly.

Botty rule no 12:

"The first thing that super successful business owners do every morning is the most critical, most important thing for the success of their business... it's marketing"

If you concentrate on doing the most important tasks first, then everything else you do in the day is a bonus. What's more, if something calamitous does occur, you'll already be ahead of the game and be able to deal with it safe in the knowledge that your business is still on track.

OK, so what else can you do to help you get more of the right things done? Who answers your phone? Who does your book-keeping? Who does your gardening? Who cleans your house? If the answer to any of these questions, is 'you', then you'll need to seriously rethink your strategy. I bet if we were to work out the numbers in your business and what you need to be earning as an hourly rate to get the life you've outlined in the goals section, you'd need to earn well above the rate you'd pay to anyone doing your book-keeping, gardening, call answering or cleaning. The 'opportunity cost' of the time taken to do these chores far outweighs the value of the tasks.

You could be spending time creating more customers for the business or creating premium pricing strategies instead. To assist you with this, Virtual Assistants (VAs) are great value and can do many things in your business that will take a lot of time, energy and focus.

Technology has given us the ability to share tasks easily using cloud-based application such as Google Drive and Dropbox. Get your VA to use a cloud based appointment planner such as Timely (http://www.gettimely.com/) or SimplyBookMe (https://simplybook.me). This will also give a better impression to prospective customers than answering the phone yourself as the business owner. Speaking of appointments, it's best to cluster these together instead of spreading them out through the day. Not only does this free up some of your time, but it also gets you to focus when you are in the meeting. Deadlines work brilliantly to focus your attention and there's no better example of this than in a short meeting with a clear objective. We find that 20 minute one-to-one sessions are far more effective than 60 minute calls. Both parties realise that there's no time to 'chat', so we get straight to the point of the call and start to make immediate progress.

We're going to talk about how you can amplify your product or service to the right audience in the next chapter using, amongst other things, the power of social media. This is a tricky one when it comes to time management, as there are no quick wins and you'll need a good strategy to be able to maximise its usage. You'll see how it fits into the Success Formula as we go through it, but for now, just remember that if you can focus and get the right things done, success will surely follow. If your tasks are aligned with your purpose, you will succeed. If your purpose is strong enough to drive you through the tough times, progression is inevitable, but if you don't make the decision to get things done, your time will get filled with other activities, which aren't going to drive you forward.

Remember, the choices you make will define your success, so choose wisely!

CASE STUDY: RACHAEL NAYLOR: THE VOICEOVER NETWORK

As a mother of two young children (a 4 year old and a 3 month old baby), I am also a busy voiceover artist, actress and the owner and founder of The VoiceOver Network, a membership organisation that offers advice, training and networking opportunities to voiceover artists at all levels. People often ask me how do I get it all done? How is it that some people seem to be able to do much more than others, when we all have the same 60 seconds in a minute, the same 60 minutes in an hour, and the same 24 hours in a day?! Well, for me it starts with goals. Set your reason for getting out of bed first and then figure out your why. Why are you doing what you're doing and where do you want to go? It makes it easier when you have clear goals and also something exciting and clear to aim for.

For me a big change came in my life when I decided I was tired of just 'getting by'. I wanted to achieve great things and have an exciting life, so I decided to stop waiting for things to happen and I made things happen. I started by setting clear goals, figuring out what I wanted my life to look like in the future and then I looked at the successful people around me and noticed that there was something they were all saying... a lot. There was something that all these people had in common. One of these people was a highly successful Entrepreneur himself; Nigel Botterill.

He spoke about 'waiting for success' versus 'making success' happen. He kept repeating how important it is to be doing your 90 minutes every day. Your 90 minutes is a special time in the day where you switch your phone and e-mails off, shut yourself away from any distractions and spend time working 'on' your business. You spend time focusing on the important things to move your business forward. However, 90 minutes seemed incredibly hard for me as a mother with a 2 year old at the time. I had such a limited amount of spare time to work with during the day, which I only managed when my little girl slept, so where would I find an extra 90 minutes a week, let alone in one day!

Anyone who has children knows that a house with a 2 year old is not a quiet place, so I looked at my day and figured out that the only way I could find any extra time was to get up at 5am and do my

90 minutes then, before my little girl woke up. So I started on the 2nd January 2014. I set my alarm and woke up super early.

To start with I found getting up this early very hard indeed. It was dark, I was so tired and it felt really odd. But it's very quiet at 5am, even in London and just like any new thing, when you start it can be tough, but keep going and they always get easier. After a while I started to understand why those 90 minutes were so important, I started to enjoy that amazing quiet time in the mornings before my little girl woke up and I became 'mum'. It's amazing how much you can get done when you don't have any distractions. After a while I didn't even need my alarm, I'd wake at 5am and jump out of bed ready to get started. When I told people what I was up to, they would look at me like I was mad! *"You get up at 5am? You're crazy!"* But I started to realise that although I appeared to be crazy, actually I was being really savvy and I was adding a whole extra day's work into my week, 4 days in a month and an extra 48 days a year! 48 incredibly productive and focused days where I worked on my business, making sure it was heading in the right direction.

I compare getting up at 5am to running in the rain, which is another thing I also enjoy. When you go for a run in the rain, very few other people are doing it. It's incredibly refreshing and when you get home afterwards you always feel amazing because you haven't been beaten by the weather. I feel the same about waking up early. Not many other people do it but you are beating that feeling of being out of control with time. It's empowering and I highly recommend it.

Things I do in my 90 minutes every morning include marketing, planning, PR, writing, strategising the company growth and as I mentioned before, I spend the time working on my business and not in it - so no checking emails or being reactive to other people's requests.

My life and business in the last couple of years has changed massively. I am doing things now I never would have dreamt of doing a few years ago. I put this down to getting my goals sorted and setting my alarm to 5am every day and doing my 90 minutes, without fail.

Life is such an amazing gift, enjoy the journey and if you want to get more out of it, you always have a choice, it's up to you.

www.thevoiceovernetwork.co.uk

ELEMENT SEVEN:
AMPLIFICATION: GETTING SOCIAL AND THE POWER OF AMAZON

"Simplify, then amplify" - Sir Richard Branson

A few years ago, Nige was invited by Sir Richard Branson to Necker Island in the British Virgin Isles. They spent some time over lunch discussing entrepreneurship and something that Sir Richard said that day, stuck with him. He said that all he did with his successful Virgin companies, was 'simply and amplify'. Virgin Airways is *all* about customer service. They took one aspect of travelling by plane (which only came about after a trip where Sir Richard had a bad customer experience) and amplified it.

This is why we looked at niching earlier on. It's all very well to be OK at most things, but much easier to find the customers who get what you do really well, especially if you are exceptional at it. It's one of the reasons I tell my clients to go and win some awards. Once you have recognition from your peers, it's proof that you are what you say you are. Great at customer service...? Go and win some awards for it then. A fantastic business enabler...? Prove it, with an award! And of course, once you do get the recognition, it's time to make some noise about it and there's no better place to do this than on *social media*.

Social Media is often misunderstood by business owners. Some think it's a total waste of time and others want to try all of it. Neither of these approaches is correct. I used to work for advertising agencies and we would often be asked by our clients to set up their social media channels for them. We'd ask them why they needed to be on social media and they usually said: *"Because everyone else is doing it,"* so we told them to go away and come back when they had a proper reason!

The clue is in the word: 'social'. It's a place where people hang out and discuss things, and as such, it's an amazing place to get into the conversation. If your company is making any impact in the marketplace, then people will be talking about you, good and bad... and it's better to be 'in' the conversation than 'out' of it. After all, if you know what is going wrong, you can do something about it and make it better - and if you know what is going right, you can tell more people about it.

The world of social media is a highly engaged global marketplace at the tip of your fingers. You can reach millions of potential customers within seconds if you know what you're doing. This chapter is going to help you understand the power of amplification through social media and give you a strategy to take your product or service to a global audience. It's also going to tell you about an often misunderstood search engine called 'Amazon' and how you can amplify your brand worldwide through writing a book. But let's first get started with the power of social.

First up, you'll need some sort of social strategy. As with everything we have talked about so far, clarity is what you are after, so start by clarifying your business's social media goals. What are you hoping to achieve by taking on a social media strategy? It's a part of your strategy that can take up a great deal of time with seemingly no returns, so you'll need to be in it for the long game...

"When I hear people debate the ROI of social media, it makes me remember why so many businesses

fail. Most are not playing the marathon, they're playing the sprint..." - Gary Vaynerchuk

You'll want to start by auditing your current social media status so you can understand your numbers going forward. You'll want to develop a 'content' strategy - we've already discussed the power of using content to educate and entertain, before you even considering selling anything - so preparing a content calendar will be essential. You'll also need to use analytics to track your progress and adjust your strategy as needed. Google provide useful social media tracking templates, which have already been created.

If you're not already on the leading 'personal relationship network', Facebook, it's time to hop on board. Even if your customers are not prevalent on this social platform, there are other tools in Facebook, which you can use to understand your potential customers' behaviours. The search bar at the top of the page for instance, is called 'graph search'. It's got immense power with a stack of data to back up its findings. Facebook changed their privacy settings a while back and unless you were savvy enough to this change, absolutely everything you do on Facebook is tracked. In some cases, what you do when you come off Facebook and onto the rest of the internet. Every time you like a page or a post, every page you visit and all of your surfing behaviours go to build up a profile of who you, and people like you, are and what you do online. If you type into the graph search, 'pages liked by people who like yoga' for instance, you'll get the most liked pages of people who like yoga. You can go very deep into building up a customer avatar using Facebook. Tools such as 'audience insights' and 'custom audiences' give you incredible power in reaching very niche targets. You can then target specific avatars using Facebook ads and banner retargetting. By using something called the 'power editor' this gives you laser like targeting. So if you wanted to promote your business to say, a 46 year old Arsenal fan, who likes The Matrix, listens to HAIM, reads The Compound Effect and lives in Maidenhead in the UK... you can. I won't go into the finer details of how to use the various social media platforms and their tools here, but I will try and give you an idea about some of their capabilities and how you can use them to promote your business. In short, Facebook is an incredible tool for sharing, connecting, engaging and discovering, and ultimately targeting, with close to a billion users.

Another one of the 'biggies' is Twitter, and despite its recent decline, it's incredibly useful for building the foundations for working relationships. I was recently invited to assist in a careers event at my eldest daughter's school. I was speaking to 13 and 14 year old girls about Event Management and other potential career choices and told them that whatever path they decided to pursue, they needed to start to follow the leading companies and thought leaders within those sectors on Twitter, starting from now. By the time they get to any sort of an interview, they should know a great deal more about the company, their habits and behaviours and some of the problems they've had to face. Moreover, the company will have had years worth of potential exposure to them too. It's quite possible they will be following one another and have made contact. The foundations have been laid. If they were really savvy, they would start to act in an entrepreneurial way, such as putting on events at their school and showing how they'd learned lessons from the experience as a result. There's no excuse for anyone leaving school to not be able to put at least some experience on their CV... if they begin to '*think*' differently. The same rules apply to everyone, it doesn't matter how old or young you are.

We had a member recently who described the powerful benefits of using Twitter when she said that, although the amount of followers they had were only just in three figures, they were highly engaged with them. It's also worth mentioning here that some larger companies still have the CEO in charge of the Twitter feed, as they've seen the potential damage of handing this over to junior employees. She said that for any 'cold calls', because the prospect already followed their feed and saw what they were up to, by the time they actually called them, it was like they already knew them and were happy to talk like friends!

I also have a neat Twitter trick, which I use to get more exposure for my books. I've set up a public list called: '*Life Changing Authors*' and add people whose books I've read which have had a profound effect on me. I'll post short excerpts from them to my followers, and because the author gets informed of my list and the posts, they invariably follow me back. After a while, I'll post a tweet with a quote from one of my books, and because of the power of reciprocation, they re-tweet this to their followers. Usually, they will have many more than me and straight away, I'll see an increase in followers (and often sales too!). So Twitter is just one example of how you can reach a very large audience, very quickly. All you need is one post, re-tweeted by someone like Sir Richard Branson and the attention you'll receive will be huge!

Whatever social media you decide to use to amplify your brand, it'll be wise to follow the 'Rule of Thirds'. Put simply, this means posting one third of your own original content, one third of aggregated, re-purposed content from thought leaders in your sector and one third content about you and your business. We all still do business with people we know, like and trust and this is 'social' media don't forget, so giving people glimpses into the real you behind the brand is really valuable.

Whatever you do, in whatever sector you are in, you can make a graphical representation of the positive change you make. A ten step guide to anything can be turned into an infographic, which can then be posted and shared on platforms such as Pinterest and Instagram. The more useful and better designed it is, the more traction it will get. You'll also need people to be able to find it, so 'tagging' and 'hash-tagging' images properly is key. However, quick tip here... don't overuse the hash-tagging feature. There's nothing worse than seeing hardly any content and a whole list of hash-tags. Of course, if your product or service is very visually based, then these platforms will be an absolute must. Pinterest is often used as a 'shop window' by users, creating lists of items they want to buy, so you'll want good quality images and links back to your own website. If you are pinning someone else's content, it's worth checking the original source and linking back to this, as this is considered the etiquette.

LinkedIn is often thought of as the professional social media platform, so it's worthwhile spending some time on making this look and feel professional. It's a superb multi-media platform and a great way to connect to business people globally. Make sure your headline and profile has the right keywords that your customers are looking for. We had a member come to our LinkedIn training day and during the morning session, he updated his header and profile and added in a service which they had recently started offering. He sent notifications to his connections before going to lunch and when he returned had a great big smile on his face. *"Well that was a worthwhile morning,"* he said, *"I've just received a £25,000 order from a current customer who called me during lunch after he'd received my update. Looks like he was trying to find a supplier and didn't realise that we offered this service - and as he already knows us...!"* Make sure you have the right profile keywords so your customers can find you and are kept up to date on what you do. LinkedIn is also a great place to find out more about your customers and potential prospects by looking in depth at their profiles and the groups they belong to. By being active in these groups, you can keep in contact with people who aren't necessarily connections. It's an excellent platform to harvest leads, solve problems, add value and share content, and you can also recommend people with whom you've had a business connection.

Video marketing is incredibly powerful, as it uses graphics and audio both at the same time. In case you didn't know, Google owns YouTube, so having content on this platform will help improve your SEO rankings. Google's aim is to provide the best possible search results for its customers, and if there is a decent video version showing an answer to someone's search query, it will value this above a text only version. Your videos will need to be watched all the way through, otherwise Google and YouTube will think they are not very good, so making the viewer watch the entire video is paramount. How can you do this? In short, keep your videos interesting! It doesn't matter if they are 30 seconds or 30 minutes, if the content is good quality and gives the viewer something in return for their time, it will be watched. Again, use the proper tagging for people to find the videos. By showing your audience how you can help them in video format, you are not only giving them quality content, but you are also showing them who *you* are too. This face to face interaction, albeit digitally, is very valuable as they get to see and engage with the real you. With the current crop of smart-phones, the quality of personal videos is now very high. You will have to think about the audio quality though, as often this is not very good on phones. Audacity is a free and simple to use audio editing platform with which you can cut, crop and improve your audio tracks.

Having your own blog is a great way to create relevant content for your target market. It helps drive traffic to your website because you are writing about your subject area and using keywords regularly which will be picked up on search engines, especially when amplified through social media channels. By adding lead generation 'calls to action' to your blog, you can use it to capture data and build your lists. An example would be: *'To find out more and get regular updates on this subject, please enter your name and email here'*. By writing regular blog posts on your specialist niche, you are positioning yourself as an authority in the process and as this content is always active, it will be picked up on search engines for years to come, especially if you get comments and interaction on the posts. Use the Google Plus social platform to post articles and blogs, as these get search priority on Google. Podcasts and webinars are also a great way to keep evergreen content on your subject matter.

Although you can use platforms such as Hootsuite, Social Oomph and Buffer to help automate your posts, it's worth pointing out that too many people automate most of their posts and responses, so it feels like you're not actually interacting with anyone. Responding quickly to comments can reap dividends... after all, social media is a two way channel!

Real time marketing social media platforms like

Snapchat, Periscope, Meerkat and Blab are all the rage at the moment, as they offer impromptu Q&A sessions, live group support, the ability to show off product features, insider views and priority announcements, and are totally live! If you can't be there in person, this is the next best thing...

Other uses for social media are emerging all of the time with developments in technology, such as real time online reviews and discussions forums, social bookmarking (Pinterest being a good example of this), niche based networks and the emergence of E-commerce as part of the whole social package. Yes, social media is more about being social than selling, but we're all busy, and as part of our desire to seek social proof, why not give the viewer the ability to buy from you in the process?

Of course, measuring the effectiveness of your social media is crucial so you'll know what to adjust or perhaps even stop doing, going forward. You'll want to focus on quality over quantity, so just getting large numbers of people to follow you is nowhere near as useful as getting the 'right' people following and *engaging* with you. I've seen business owners putting too much emphasis on the clicks, rather than the click-throughs and conversions. A simple mistake to make, so be warned.

One last piece of advice on social is to always keep your target audience in mind and don't ever badmouth your competition or get into fights with people who disagree with you. I've never seen this come to any good, just acknowledge it and move on. Of course, if they are picking up something that needs addressing, by all means address it and show how you've learned as a result... then move on.

So let's now look at the power of Amazon.

I often get criticised in trainings for going on and on about becoming an author, but I can't emphasise enough the value that it brings to amplifying your brand and your business success. My first book: Do Nothing! has been the engine room of my business success over the last few years, as well as being responsible for changing the lives of many of its readers. I'm hoping this book will also have an impact on a lot of you too by the way.

A book is a perfect way to condense what you know into a great little package, which will get read by a global marketplace. This is because Amazon is actually a *search engine*. Just like YouTube, LinkedIn and Google Plus, Amazon carries a lot of weight with Google, who want to provide good quality content for their customers. A well written book, full of the keywords your customer is searching for, does just that. So how do you go about writing one then...?

"The key to writing a book is to 'Just Write!' Writing is one thing that you cannot get worse at by doing it."
- Brian Tracey

T.S. Eliot worked full time at a bank. His biographer, Peter Ackroyd, said, *"He would try to rise two hours earlier than was strictly necessary in order to concentrate upon his own writing, and then he would travel to the bank."* Stephen King writes 2000 words every day, and if you only wrote 500 words a day, you would have a book within a few months. The best way to learn to write, is to write and write and write and on the book writing courses which I run, I get attendees to promise to write a minimum of 500 words every day for 3 months. The trick is to not do the editing part until you've managed to get all the words down on paper (or digitally) first.

Of course, you'll need to find something to write

about, so start with a message, idea, or story that you really want to share with others or something that's going to add value to your brand. This *must* be something for which you have an absolute passion, something which you truly believe in, or even some knowledge or expertise you've collected that will benefit the lives of others. Being an expert on your subject matter and showing your expertise as an authority in your field is the point of this exercise, so if you want to write about success, you must be successful. If you want to write about money, you must already have some and if you want to write about relationships, you must not have been divorced seventeen times!

Then, as we did for your business ideas in the very beginning, think about your target customers. What are their interests and concerns? What are the problems that they have which your book will ultimately solve? What are the frustrations that your book will take away from them? Make a list of 20-30 thoughts, ideas, stories and insights which you could include in your book.

Next, look on Amazon and find out what are the three top selling books in your desired category or which solve your problem, and then list three differences that your book offers to your readers that these books don't - in other words, why is your book different?

Get together all the information and research that you will need to write your book. Do you have examples and experiences, which explain and back up each of your 20-30 points? If not, what pieces are you missing and where might you find these?

Think about what will be contained in each chapter and how these will be organised in relationship to each other. Make a list of 7-10 chapter titles where you will break down your main subject into smaller headings. The book you are reading right now has been put together in this precise manner, so use it as an example. Then make a list of ideas you would write about if you were commissioned to write a minimum of 2,500 words. This is a great way of finding out what you will be interested enough to write about in the coming weeks and months ahead.

As you write, keep expanding your knowledge on the subject matter. I had to rewrite my first book three times as I learned more and more about the subject matter and my own thinking changed as a result.

Once you have your list of ideas and chapter headings, start writing. Here is one way to overcome 'writer's block' that works every time: when you can't think of anything to write, just start writing: *"I don't know what to write... I don't know what to write..."* Believe me, by the time you write this three times, your brain will give you something to write about!

I always like to start with a powerful opening sentence that immediately grabs the reader's attention, but don't get too concerned if this doesn't come to you straight away, it will come eventually. Even Ernest Hemingway said: *"The first draft of anything is sh*t."*

Based on the planning you've already done, you should be getting an idea of how you can add to this outline and write the main content required for your book. In my own experience, the best way to do this is to keep writing, writing and writing some more, until you feel that most of your ideas are 'downloaded'. Only then can you start to edit and organise. Many people fail to complete the books they start when they get bogged down in the editing stage without finishing the downloading part first. The introduction, preface and acknowledgments come later, so don't worry about these parts yet.

Of course, you could get someone to write the book for you as an option, especially if you have very little time to spare. Dictating a book and getting someone to transcribe the audio is another option. However you choose to do the writing part, just make sure that you are consistent. Remember, it's who you become as part of the process that is key here. Don't get down on yourself if you fail to write everyday, just get back into the swing of it as soon as you can.

I stumbled across my own writing formula by chance and I remember attending an author's conference once where I sat next to a lady who'd also written a book... on how to write a book. When I told her my own story, about getting everything down on paper (or computer) first and not editing it, she told me she'd have to add in another chapter to include my method! Most importantly, it works. We've had dozens of published authors and best sellers come through the book writing course and there are more planned for the future, so if you want some accountability, book onto one of them here: ECTrainingAcademy.org

We'll tell you all about how to publish your own title (or even get yourself a literary agent), and how to market and sell your book to maximise amplification.

There are tips and tricks about using Kindle to maximise reviews and reach, the best ways to design your book cover so it sells well, how to make the most out of your Amazon page and price your book correctly - including how to use a free pricing strategy for maximum sales. We also cover publicity, where to get your book featured and which online and offline publications to ask for reviews.

On the basis that your social media and book writing strategy is going to amplify your products and services to a much wider audience, there's a good chance that you're going to need some help soon on your journey, so the next chapter is all about how to find and keep the right people for your mission.

CASE STUDY: ANDREW AND CLAIRE BOWEN FROM THE CAFESUCCESSHUB

The Daily Grind Book, Case Study

The idea of starting our coffee shop support membership website, Cafesuccesshub, was to share the knowledge and experience that we had both acquired through running our coffee shop business Java&Co. We had become used to coaching new coffee shop start-ups informally, so getting everything into one place was a logical progression.

As a way of publicising the website and positioning and asserting our authority in our market, we decided that we should write a book, but we just had no idea how to do it.

Signing up for the book writing training course with Damian was therefore an easy decision to make and we were delighted that after six months we had a draft copy in our hands, something that we are very proud of.

The first part of the course, in April 2015, was a real eye opener on many levels, but the key mantra was 'write five hundred words each day for five months and you will have a book'.

We were fortunate to have so many focused and determined individuals in one room on that day, helping each other formulate a vision, a title and a deadline. The passion to get a book published forced us all to commit to a follow up meeting, which we could only take part in, if we had a physical copy. That was a major incentive to get it completed.

At the first course everyone had a plethora of questions; how to design a cover? How to take the book to print? How to get an ISBN number? How many chapters to write? How long should the book be? How do we publicise and promote it? Although all of these questions were addressed, our focus was directed towards doing creative writing and not worrying about the finer details too soon. Because Damian had already published a best selling book, he knew the subject inside and out and was an authority in his own right.

We discovered that getting our book printed was actually very easy and cheap. Using Lulu.com was straightforward, with any queries being addressed online without the need to talk to anyone and three days after uploading our book, it landed on the doormat!

Unusually (as we later found out), Claire and I were writing the book together, so we had to develop a way of collaborating. We produced an outline of the book as a mind-map, which provided the structure, flow and style and then bounced drafts back and forth using a Dropbox folder. One of us was more creative early in the day and the other later at night, which allowed us to work more effectively as a team throughout the day.

The private Facebook group we joined following the course was also a fantastic motivator, sounding board, 'conscience' and help-line all in one. Seeing what other writers in the group had achieved each day certainly encouraged a level of friendly rivalry!

The public declaration of our deadline for publication, through setting up a pre-order page on the dailygrindbook.com and telling everyone we knew that we were writing a book, was another reason why we could not fail to achieve our objective. When we went on to pre-sell books to people all over the world, there was simply no turning back.

The reaction from people changed after about five months. We stopped saying that we were writing a book and started saying that we had written it. The process of editing however, took longer than we had anticipated. Getting it proofread by a third party was essential. You become blind to your own words after a while and miss so many obvious mistakes and typos.

Out of the 32 people who attended the course 12

attended the follow up course in October with their book in hand, which was an amazing conversion rate.

Planning the launch, getting PR and asking for a foreword from someone we respected were all done whilst we were writing, to ensure that we were ready for publication.

Our book came out as promised and on time, in December 2015 and is proving to be such a valuable asset in our business. The feedback has been fantastic and the feeling of being published authors is absolutely wonderful.

www.cafesuccesshub.com

ELEMENT EIGHT: NO ONE CAN DO IT ALONE: ATTRACTING AND KEEPING SUPERSTARS

"Hire people who are better than you are, then leave them to get on with it. Look for people who will aim for the remarkable, who will not settle for the routine."

\- David Ogilvy

Let me start this chapter by telling you a story from the book *'Start with Why'* by Simon Sinek, essential reading for every new member of the Entrepreneurs Circle: *[Published with kind permission from the author].*

Early in the twentieth century, the English adventurer Ernest Shackleton set out to explore the Antarctic. Roald Amundsen, a Norwegian, had only just become the first explorer ever to reach the South Pole, leaving one remaining conquest: the crossing of the continent via the southernmost tip of the Earth.

The land part of the expedition would start at the Frigid Weddell Sea, below South America, and travel

1,700 miles across the pole to the Ross Sea, below New Zealand. The cost, Shackleton estimated at the time, would be about $250,000. "The crossing of the South Polar continent will be the biggest polar journey ever attempted," Shackleton told a reporter for the New York Times on December 29, 1913. "The unknown fields in the world which are still unconquered are narrowing down, but there still remains this great work."

On December 5, 1914, Shackleton and a crew of twenty-seven men set out for the Weddell Sea on the Endurance, a 350-ton ship that had been constructed with funds from private donors, the British Government and the Royal Geographical Society. By then, World War One was raging in Europe, and money was growing more scarce. Donations from English schoolchildren paid for the dog teams. But the crew of the Endurance would never reach the continent of Antarctica.

Just a few days out of South Georgia Island in the Southern Atlantic, the ship encountered mile after mile of pack ice, and was soon trapped as winter moved in early and with fury. Ice closed in around the ship "Like an almond in a piece of toffee," a crew member wrote.

Shackleton and his crew were stranded in the Antarctic for ten months as the Endurance drifted slowly north, until the pressure of the ice floes finally crushed the ship. On November 21, 1915, the crew watched as she sank in the frigid waters of the Weddell Sea.

Stranded on the ice, the crew of the Endurance boarded their three lifeboats and landed on tiny Elephant Island. There, Shackleton left behind all but five of his men and embarked on a hazardous journey across 800 miles of rough seas to find help. Which, eventually, they did.

What makes the story of the Endurance so remarkable, however, is not the expedition, it's that throughout the whole ordeal - no one died, there were no stories of people eating others and no mutiny. This was not luck. This was because Shackleton hired good fits. He found the right men for the job. When you fill an organisation with good fits, those who believe what you believe, success just happens. And how did Shackleton find this amazing crew? With a simple ad in the London Times.

Compare that to how we hire people. Like Shackleton, we run ads in the newspaper, or on the modern equivalents, Craigslist or Monster.com.

Sometimes we hire a recruiter to find someone for us, but the process is largely the same. We provide a list of qualifications for the job and expect that the best candidate will be the one who meets those requirements.

The issue is how we write those ads. They are all about what - and not about why. A 'what' ad might say, for example, "Account executive needed, minimum five years' experience, must have working knowledge of industry. Come and work for a fantastic, fast growing company with great pay and great benefits." The ad may produce loads of applicants, but how do we know which is the right fit?

Shackleton's ad for crew members was different. His did not say what he was looking for. His ad did not say: "Men needed for expedition. Minimum five years' experience. Must know how to hoist mainsail. Come work for a fantastic captain."

Rather, Shackleton was looking for those with something more. He was looking for a crew that belonged on such an expedition. His actual ad ran like this:

"Men wanted for hazardous journey. Small wages, bitter cold, long months of complete darkness, constant

danger, safe return doubtful. Honour and recognition in case of success."

The only people who applied for the job were those who read the ad and thought it sounded great. They loved insurmountable odds. The only people who applied for the job were survivors. Shackleton hired only people who believed what he believed. Their ability to survive was guaranteed.

When employees belong, they will guarantee your success. And they won't be working hard and looking for innovative solutions for you, they will be doing it <u>for themselves</u>.

Now it's worth reading that last bit again. If you can find the people who *believe in what you believe*, then they will move Heaven and Earth to help you. You might now see why we spent so long on the first two chapters and why this is so important. If you haven't completed the exercises in the previous chapters as suggested, now's the time to go back and do them... please!

"Two-thirds of workers under 30 don't think they're in the right career yet and more than half expect to

undergo a career change within two years"
- Source: Harris poll 2014

With figures like this, how is it possible to attract not only the right staff, but the very best staff to your business?

When you can create a culture and a set of values that will help you to get the very best work out of the very best people (just like the Entrepreneurs Circle has done), your business has a great chance of being in that small percentage that thrives in the early stages.

To attract the right people to your business, you need to break out of the old thinking of 'work for work's sake' and adopt the Steve Jobs mentality of 'Making a dent on the Universe'. Instead, one simple way to do this is to compare 'task' versus 'purpose'. There is an old story about three bricklayers, who were working side by side on a wall. A passer-by approached the first one and asked, *"What are you doing?"* The first bricklayer responded, *"What do you think I'm doing? I'm laying bricks!"* They asked the second bricklayer, *"What are you doing?"* The second bricklayer responded, *"Can't you see what I'm doing? I'm building a wall!"* Finally, they went to the last bricklayer and asked, *"What are you doing?"* and he responded, *"I am building a cathedral!"*

All three bricklayers answered the same question correctly. The first one was laying bricks, true; the second one answered that he was building a wall, also true; but how come the third one saw a cathedral where his colleagues saw only bricklaying and wall building?

When you have no clear vision of where the end is and what it means, all you do is busy activity, producing nothing of real value. *Vision* is what makes your activity meaningful. For these three brickies, who do you think would be more motivated? The first two are the people who say, 'life is hard'. They are in an activity that seems to be going nowhere, so they get easily frustrated and discouraged.

Start to think about your own business in visionary terms, whatever those may be to you, and then think about how to communicate these beliefs and values to your team.

Do the following exercise, called the 'Five Whys'? Start with the statement: We make X products or we deliver X services. Then ask yourself: 'Why is this important?' five times. After one or two whys, you'll find that you're getting down to the fundamental purpose of your product, service or organisation.

Your core purpose is your organisation's reason for being. An effective purpose reflects your employees' motivations for doing their work. It doesn't just describe the organisation's output or target customers; it captures the very *soul* of the organisation. An example of a successful global brand which adopts and cultivates this approach would be Disney: Disney's Core Purpose is *'To make people happy'*.

But imagine if Walt Disney had conceived of his company's purpose was to make cartoons, rather than to make people happy; we probably wouldn't have Disneyland today!

Core values are therefore the timeless guiding principles in an organisation which require no external justification, as they have intrinsic value and importance to all those inside the company. Disney's core values of imagination and wholesomeness stem not from a market requirement but from Walt Disney's own beliefs that imagination and wholesomeness should be nurtured for its own sake.

Great companies decide what values they hold true, independent of the current environment. There are no universally 'correct' set of core values but companies tend to have only a few - as only a few values can be truly core - that is, so deeply held that they will never change. Disney's Core Values are; No cynicism; Nurturing and promulgation of 'wholesome American values'; Creativity, dreams, and imagination; Fanatical attention to consistency and detail; and Preservation and control of the Disney magic.

Zappos is another company who also holds core values that guide their super success on a global scale. In 1998, Zappos.com founder Nick Swinmurn went shopping in San Francisco looking for a particular pair of shoes. One shop had the right style, but not the right colour. Another had the right colour, but not the right size. Nick spent the next hour walking from shop to shop, finally going home empty-handed and frustrated. He didn't have any more luck when he arrived home, because although there were a lot of shops selling shoes online, there were no major online retailers that specialised in selling *only* shoes. Seeing both a need and an opportunity, Nick resigned from his job and started Shoesite.com.

Nick wanted the business to be able to expand into other product categories, so Shoesite.com needed a name change. *"Nick also asked me what I thought of*

'Zapos' as the name for the company, derived from zapatos, which was the Spanish word for 'shoes,'" recalls Zappos CEO Tony Hsieh. *"I told him that he should add another p to it so that people wouldn't mispronounce it and accidentally say ZAY-pos."* Zappos.com was born.

Today's Zappos offerings continue to evolve and include clothing, accessories, housewares and beauty, with more in the pipeline. Whilst the original idea was to offer the best online selection, something happened to sharpen the company's mission. That something was what is now known as the first 'WOW letter'.

In January of 2000, a customer emailed to describe her Zappos shopping experience. She tried ordering two different pairs of shoes, both of which were unavailable - but that wasn't why she contacted them. It was the fast, courteous response of the Zappos Customer Loyalty Team as well as receiving both a gift certificate and a T-shirt for the inconvenience that WOW'ed her. This feedback changed everything for Zappos: What if the company focused not solely on what it sold, but *how* it sold it? What if Zappos focused on WOW-ing its customers? *"We asked ourselves what we wanted this company to stand for,"* said CEO

Tony Hsieh, *"We didn't want to sell just shoes. I wasn't even into shoes - but I was passionate about customer service."* Do you see now why your 'why' can and should change as you evolve?

As Zappos grew, it became important to find a way to maintain this new culture with each new recruit. In January of 2005, Zappos polled every employee on what they thought their core values should be. Of the 37 suggestions, 10 Core Values were chosen and continue to guide the Zappos culture today in everything from hiring to firing. The 10 Core Values are:

1. Deliver WOW Through Service
2. Embrace and Drive Change
3. Create Fun and A Little Weirdness
4. Be Adventurous, Creative, and Open-Minded
5. Pursue Growth and Learning
6. Build Open and Honest Relationships with Communication
7. Build a Positive Team and Family Spirit
8. Do More With Less
9. Be Passionate and Determined
10. Be Humble

Zappos culture and values are the fundamental driver of its success and attraction of new talent. Rather than focusing on 'what it does', it's a shift to 'why and how it does it' that makes Zappos stand out.

Corporate culture happens as soon as there are more than just you in the office. It's not so much a question of 'whether' your business has a corporate culture, but a question of 'what kind' of corporate culture it has or is going to have going forward. This culture is the system of values and beliefs that your business holds, which drives actions, behaviours and relationships.

On that basis, is your corporate culture one that 'just happens' or one that is established, by design? Is it one that is open to interpretation or one that is well defined? Is it one that is vague or one that is crystal clear, one that lacks purpose or one that is goal or result oriented? Whatever your answers to these questions, now's the time to think about HOW to develop your company's core culture and values.

Decide if you are committed to running a 'values-based' company - you might simply be in it to make a quick buck. If so, you won't attract the best people to your business, only those who are also only interested in the money. On the basis you want a company culture not based on money alone, then figure out your own personal values and beliefs first. Be honest. Review the significant milestones in your life and/or life-changing events and see how these affect your life now and what you believe in as a result. If you have others already in the business, get their values and beliefs - key partners, managers, and/or any influencers you may have - and combine them with your own.

Test your commitment by asking yourself if you would be willing to hire and fire people based on whether they fit your core values, even if that employee adds a lot of value in the short-term? If the answer is yes, integrate your core values into everything you do, especially hiring, firing, and performance reviews. Your company or corporate culture is just the way that people in your business 'do things', and a positive and productive corporate culture isn't going to happen by accident. It's YOUR business, it's YOUR responsibility.

Once you have your values, you'll need to select the right people and offer training for consistent quality. Your own internal communication should be to inform and inspire and to create an environment of care about your values.

So how do Disney use their core values to attract the right staff? In a survey of over 2,000 job seekers conducted by Monster, three quarters said that they regularly see jargon or acronyms in job postings, and more than half say that this puts them off from applying for a job at all. There are a number of things that must be done right in the beginning of the hiring process because they cannot be repaired later on and one of the biggest mistakes organisations make is being too casual at this crucial stage.

Disney believe that every applicant comes to them with pre-existing skills and behaviours - some that match their requirements and some that do not. These skills and behaviours will vary based on the values of every organisation; however, there are certain things that can be done to increase the likelihood of hiring people with a propensity to be great. In the job description, include the skills and behaviours that the best employee for the job would need to have. Use behaviourally based questions as a part of the interview process (How would you respond if...?). Pepper in questions that test for cultural values by listening for key repeatable messages from the applicant: *"You mentioned the customer experience several times in your response, can you explain what makes this so important to you?"*

Disney also offers an explicit description of the company's culture and values in each job description, such as, *"As a Cast Member you are the steward and connection to our legacy and the backbone of our thriving innovations. Join our team and watch your dreams come true."* This signals to the applicant that the heritage of our company is something to be held in high regard, and that this person would be charged with helping to uphold that ideal. Do the same in your organisation!

Like Disney, the Entrepreneurs Circle hire for attitude, more than skills or experience. These play a part, but we want to find the *right* people who fit our culture, as we can probably teach them everything they need to know. It's not so much what they can do and more about who they ARE!

Most people join our team through the 'group interview' process. There's a group of interviewees and a group of interviewers - both are important factors, and so is our process. Here it is:

1.   Start them early in our office (say 7am)
2.   Tell us something about the company

(everyone should know at least something!)

3. Show us how you work as a team (eg: role playing)
4. Tell us a little about you and what makes you interesting
5. Semi-formal interview
6. Live test of some sort

Then if you want to be really sneaky, add in one or more of the following:

7. Set up an angry customer scenario to see how they react to a difficult situations
8. Create a trick emergency, such as a broken laptop or a fake fire alarm

If you've recruited people with the right attitude, training them should be the easy bit. We set out the parameters, but hand a great deal of responsibility and autonomy back to staff members. The right people will feel empowered and embrace this. We paint a big picture of our business and where we're heading to all our employees. We share our plans and ambitions with them so they can choose to help us on the journey. Without an understanding at some level of the bigger picture, an employee is much less likely to add value and succeed in their role. It's a simply case of 'task' versus 'purpose'.

We then aim to get the best out of the right people by using a *cycle of excellence*, which works by exploiting the power of the interaction between what is within them and what lies outside of them. Neither the individual nor the job, holds the magic. But the right person doing the right job creates the magical interaction that leads to peak performance and incredible results. Every manager has an opportunity to make this magic happen by guiding employees and putting the right people into the right roles so that their brains light up.

If you want to take it to the next level, understand that imaginative engagement catalyses work and can help people become phenomenally productive. You can create conditions where people actually want to work hard by making tasks both challenging and important, so that overcoming them is empowering to the individual. Giving recognition and noticing when a person excels is also critical and cultures that help people shine inevitably becomes a culture of self-perpetuating excellence. In short, always reward excellence!

To finish off, great businesses should set their new employees up for success by making expectations clear, reinforcing their culture and creating an emotional buy-in. The first few weeks of having someone new on board are critical, and that's where a good new-starter process pays dividends. Does every new employee have a written record of your expectations of what success looks like for them in their new role? If not, now is the right time to make one and to communicate it effectively. Some simple ways to improve communication would be to have an open door policy; semi-formal one-on-one meetings; have a private employee Facebook group; organise regular lunches and nights out or even have an anonymous suggestion box.

Positive employee attitudes result when employees know they are appreciated, and great businesses make big efforts to support employees by recognising their accomplishments, involving them in decisions and making the best use of their talents, skills and experiences. But I'll leave the final word to Sir Richard Branson from Virgin who says: *"If you treat your employees right, they will treat your customers right, and success will follow."*

CASE STUDY: KATE LESTER FROM DIAMOND LOGISTICS

Diamond Logistics employ fifteen full time staff at their head quarters in Guildford, Surrey with a further fifteen sub-contractors and two outsourced workers. They own twenty five franchises with a minimum of four employees at each site plus their subcontractors, totalling approximately 200 stakeholders within the business.

Here's Kate Lester, Diamond Logistic's CEO and founder, on how to hire and keep superstars: "A successful entrepreneur is someone who has the ability to build a sustainable and profitable business from an idea, which contributes in some way to society. You'll require incredible vision to see what your idea can develop into, as well as the guile to see the pitfalls and challenges that you'll have to face in its execution.

Then of course there's the ability to communicate in a manner that all stakeholders in the business not only understand, but will wholly subscribe to. You'll need to be a talent spotter - someone who can seek out, recruit, mentor and inspire a team to help you build your vision. You'll have to be an evangelist for your brand, someone who is able to seek out an audience who enjoy the benefits your vision will bring. Most importantly, being a successful entrepreneur is about remaining humble, because there's no 'me' in business building - it's all about 'we'. If you drill deeper - the successful entrepreneur's job is therefore all about people.

At Diamond Logistics, I am the chief talent spotter and my job is really to discover the superstars that can help me fulfill the vision. It's no accident that the upturns in our business occurred when we recruited key people - so if you want your business to be successful you need to put recruitment, management, training and retention at the heart of your organisation.

How do we do this at Diamond? By being a company people want to work for. We get plenty of approaches from job-seekers because they see where we're going and want to be a part of it. Sometimes, if the candidate is exceptional and we don't have a position available, we create one. If a resource with potential shows up, it's worth creating a role to match their talents and prevent them joining our competition. When I've taken on people we probably didn't need but could see what they might bring, we've always ended up improving as a business.

Take Dan Allin for instance. Dan came to me with a skill-set we didn't have at the time, but this ended up being a major growth area in the business as a result. I certainly didn't need another recruit then - we were looking at facilitating a merger - but when he showed up and said where he thought we were going and how he could make the business grow differently, I was intrigued. He's been pivotal to our growth and is now a director and a shareholder. All that from a highly speculative approach.

Make sure the personality of the company shines through in your recruitment adverts - talk about the type of company, the magnitude of the role and make it into a pitch for your brand. Be fussy about how candidates should apply and use this part of the process to filter out any poor applicants who can't follow instructions.

To build a sustainable business, you'll need a few plodders, the people who are prepared to do the donkey work. You also need a smattering of talent and a visionary or two. The idea is not to recruit replicas of yourself - so make sure you are not hiring anyone who you are drawn to personally. Instead, find the right shaped pieces to fit into the complicated jigsaw puzzle of your business.

In Diamond, some people commit fully from 8am to 6pm, and that's it. Their email and phones are switched off out of these hours, but for the 10 hours they are here, they give 100%. And that's fine. Others are betting their lives and career on Diamond and invest 150% - coming up with ideas outside of work, suggesting change, adding more value than their salary suggests it should. Others are fully committed but lack the strategic skills and need to be told what to do. That's okay too, but they should all be performing to their best ability. Any less than that and they're not helping you get to where you need to, but more importantly, they're taking the place of someone else who might be able to help you get there faster. You pay your staff 100% of their salary - so expect 100% performance from them.

Always make sure the reward is commensurate with the effort. Nothing p*ss*s people off more than feeling another team member is plodding along in their job and getting the same reward as someone else who's sweating blood and guts. Match the reward with effort, but most importantly, results. A fixed basic with lots of bonuses works wonders for this!

Let the team select. In the end, recruitment is about adding skills and potential to a unit - so we let our team decide. Franchises are able to vet a candidate before due diligence starts, whilst other team members come in on the final interviews. We've found this to be an excellent vetting procedure because their opinions really count. Ask the candidate to work a day for free. This is the number one tactic, which has saved us tens of thousands in poor recruits. If they're not willing to commit to just one day - then we don't want them anyway. In one day the rest of the team can get a pretty good idea of whether they're a good fit or not and we get a chance to test their skill-set too.

We also always look at individual key motivators. This might be a sense of belonging, an opportunity to grow, praise, air miles, even a job they can forget about after 6pm - but whatever it is that motivates them, a good manager will make sure this is being fulfilled in the role and their rewards. One of my team wants to be my replacement one day - and I welcome that. Others want directorships. For some it's the money. For others, it's the status. Titles and decision-making ability is also important. Some simply need the flexibility to do what they want to do outside of work. 'Different strokes for different folks' as the saying goes...

We work hard to create a sense of culture and belonging at Diamond. We're considered a bit 'Marmite' here, but that's okay. You're either a Diamond - or you're not. We have our Twelve Golden Rules up on the wall - a 'Shared Success' mantra that puts a mutually beneficial relationship at the heart of the business and a mission statement, which is repeated like a chant. People either love it, or they don't get it and they last less than 3 months or stay a lifetime. There are very few in-betweeners here at Diamond. Also, we don't call them employees, we prefer stakeholders or team members, but it's all about making it an inclusive experience. Employees say they 'give' years of their life to a business. That's not strictly true - I'm pretty sure very few work for free, but there is certainly a sacrifice being made on their part, so make it worthwhile. I believe personally in profit incentives, team benefits and even shareholding - contrary to the opinions of many entrepreneurs - but I say share as much as you can. Share success and people will give you more than you ever anticipated."

www.diamondlogistics.co.uk

Entrepreneur Success Formula

ELEMENT NINE: SUCCESS CATALYST: BEING REMARKABLE, AND WHY YOUR HEALTH REALLY MATTERS

"The remarkable thing is, we have a choice everyday regarding the attitude we will embrace for that day." -
Charles R. Swindoll

OK, so there is a secret sauce and this is it! What will make your journey that much quicker with more chance of succeeding? We've touched upon all aspects of this chapter at some stage throughout the book, but it's worth bringing them all to a crescendo here because they might well be the defining factor in your success.

It's all very well to say 'be remarkable', but what does that actually mean? Well, let's take David Costa from Flowers Unlimited, an EC member who owns and runs a chain of flower shops based around Brighton and the South East of England. Every part of the flower buying process in David's business has been designed to be remarkable.

As soon as an order is placed online, an email confirmation goes out to the buyer with a picture of the flowers, which are due to be arranged, plus a photograph of the flower arranger who will be doing the work. Once the flowers have been prepared, another email goes out to the buyer with a confirmation using a picture of the arrangement.

David's vans look remarkable, with vinyls to make them appear as if the doors are open and there are wonderful bouquets inside. The driver of the van is not called simply a 'delivery driver', they are the 'deliverer of happiness' and have been hand picked by the staff and not just by David. This is because they are the customer facing representation of the brand, so it's really important for everyone to get this person just right.

As soon as the flowers have been delivered, the buyer gets a confirmation. However this doesn't just say when they were delivered, it tells the buyer what the reaction was from the recipient. If for any reason (as often happens) they aren't at home, the deliverer of happiness will see if a neighbour is in. But of course, even this part of the process has been thought through and is remarkable. Instead of simply asking for the neighbour to take in the flowers, the deliverer of happiness will give them a 'good neighbour award' and a discount voucher.

Two days after delivery, a package will go out to the recipient of the flowers with instructions on how to make the flowers last longer, plus some more flower food and a voucher for their next order. Their staff always get superb feedback and Flowers Unlimited are now taking on more stores in the South East.

It's a fact, that if you want to stand out from the crowd, you'll need to start thinking along the same lines as David Costa and his team at Flowers Unlimited. Being remarkable (worthy of remark) should become part of your business thinking from now on.

In the chapter on mindset, I described how thought and thinking is one of the key components to entrepreneurial success and how understanding the process will help you to deal with the bumps in the road. When you see how the system works, it's so much easier to look at situations through fresh eyes and start to see everything as part of the journey, instead of good or bad.

"For there is nothing either good or bad, but thinking makes it so" - William Shakespeare

This makes it so much easier to wake up every day safe in the knowledge that whatever life throws at you, you're going to be OK and get through it, and with this knowledge to guide you, you can take on life and its challenges head on. However, to do this really effectively there is one last element in the formula that has to be put in place.

As we've already mentioned, everything you do as an entrepreneur is part of your business. Everything you eat and drink, how much you exercise and sleep you get, and all of your daily habits and behaviours, will add up over time to contribute to your overall level of your success. I recently had a conversation with an athletics coach working with the Swedish Olympic team for next year's Brazilian games. He told me that they will not work with any athlete who is still eating wheat and gluten, as this amounts to an immediate 15-20% drop in performance. The world number one tennis player, Novak Djokovic famously went a whole season unbeaten after being advised to give up wheat and gluten and he's still at the top of his game now.

Coincidence...?

There are a number of books about how damaging wheat and gluten are to our health and the scientific reasoning behind this. Wheat Belly by Dr William Davis and Grain Brain: The Surprising Truth about Wheat, Carbs, and Sugar - Your Brain's Silent Killers by Dr David Perlmutter are two very enlightening and essential reads.

I steer clear of both wheat and gluten as much as possible and have seen a massive increase in not only my mental performance but in my physical performance on the squash court as well. Weight loss has been merely a by-product of keeping clear of these two inflammatory foods.

I'd also like to personally thank some EC members, Dave Stickland, John Lamerton and Mark Chase for pointing me in the direction of the juicing expert, Jason Vale. Jason wrote a book about ten years ago, which has nothing to do with juicing but is an absolute game changer. I wasn't even aware that he'd written it until they mentioned it to me. If anyone thinks that they drink alcohol too often, get Jason's book called *'Kick the drink... easily!'* It's absolutely incredible, and although I wasn't much of a drinker anyway, I've stopped completely now. As soon as you realise how much drinking even a small amount of alcohol affects your body on a daily basis (you are drinking poison after all) you'll want to stop drinking completely too. Your sleep will improve, along with your memory, your ability to think more clearly and your physical capabilities. This will affect every area of your life and not just your business. Since I stopped a few months ago, I haven't wanted to touch alcohol, and I've actually become more sociable, not less. It's nothing to do with 'giving up' and everything to do with realising what you are doing in the first place, and the behaviour (drinking alcohol) simply not making sense anymore. Without a change in mindset, there is no change in behaviour and this book will change your thinking about drinking. I feel as though a fog has been lifted from my mind and I am able to operate at peak performance throughout the day.

Jason Vale is best known for his love and promotion of juicing, something that will also give you boundless energy and vitality. My own personal favourite is my spinach, pineapple, cucumber, carrot and banana smoothies at 10.30am instead of a mid-morning nibble on sugary snacks. It's a simple understanding that whatever you put in, you'll get the same return in performance. So if you want better performance, use better fuel!

I mentioned Hal Elrod's Miracle Morning book earlier on. If you eat and drink well, making the commitment to get up earlier to either exercise or do your 90 minutes, will be a cinch. I find it very easy now to get up at 5.30am every morning to write.

Studies have shown the benefits of regular exercise, and even going out for the occasional walk will clear your head and help you think and feel better. Try and make exercise, or at least getting some fresh air, part of your daily routine too.

Another 'life hack' I absolutely swear by, is my bulletproof coffee in the morning. Alongside my bowl of fresh fruit and gluten free granola, I make my coffee by adding some unsalted butter and a spoonful of coconut oil to my French press blend in my Breville Blend-Active, to make a creamy smooth, high performance kick-starter. Both Dave Asprey and Tim Ferriss talk extensively about the benefits of this morning drink. You'll have to do the research into the benefits of Ketones in areas such as cancer prevention and peak performance, as these are what being on a low carb diet and drinking the coffee gives you, but I'll tell you what it does for me... I am absolutely flying both mentally and physically throughout the day! And I don't even drink caffeine at all after midday but stick to the juicing to keep my energy levels up instead.

My diet consists of cutting out most carbs, all the wheat and glutens, and sticking to grass-fed meats, wild salmon and mostly green vegetables with the occasional piece of dark chocolate thrown in for desert.

It works.

Very, very well...

And of course these days, it's pretty easy to go out and get gluten and wheat free alternatives to pretty much anything, everywhere. It always comes back down to the choices you are making on a daily basis, and I've found that the more 'right thinking' I do, the easier it is to succeed. Speaking of which, did you manage to spot the 'base element' running throughout the book?

For anyone that still hasn't managed to work it out, it is of course.... your thinking! Everything you do comes down to your mindset and the thinking you act upon. The only difference between you and the most successful entrepreneurs throughout history is the thoughts they have and the thoughts you have and the ones they decided to take action on. When the thinking you pay attention to changes, your behaviours will change and your world will change as a result. Success is a series of choices made time and time again, compounding together to make your life story. Greatness is not something to be attained in the future, it is achieved in the choices we make in every moment of every day. As Michael Jackson so eloquently penned: "I'm starting with the Man in the mirror. I'm asking him to change his ways. And no message could have been any clearer: If you wanna make the world a better place, take a look at yourself, and then make a change."

I hope this book has given you some ideas and insights into how this formula works for successful entrepreneurs, what you can do to make your own entrepreneurial journey into a successful one and who you need to become to achieve it. On the following pages, there is an opportunity to continue your journey with us. So I hope to see you soon and help you to apply the Entrepreneur Success Formula to your own business and your life.

CASE STUDY: GARY FULLWOOD: WATFORD KITCHENS AND BATHROOMS

On the 20th December 2014, I sat on my showroom floor and cried. I was over £50k in debt and didn't know where my next client was coming from. I felt broken and lost. The crazy thing is, I have always been really positive but at that moment in time I needed a wake up call. After wiping the tears from my face, I stopped feeling sorry for myself and phoned a couple of friends, who in turn gave me a right boll*cking and laid the truth on the line. There is simply no point in having friends who just tell you everything is going to be OK all the time.

After those calls I stood there and looked at myself in the mirror and said: *"I am not going down like this, I'm going to find a way and I'm going to succeed."* This is where my life took a turn for the better because I realised the only way my circumstances were going to change, was if my attitude changed, so I started to create monthly, quarterly and end of year goals.

Remaining positive confused a lot of people, as they couldn't understand why and how I could stay so upbeat. But really knowing what I could achieve, albeit with some tough decisions and sacrifices, I never doubted my own ability and belief. I woke up every day telling myself how amazing I was and that anything was possible.

In October 2015, I had done it! I had created a stable business once again by putting the right systems and processes in place. I achieved my one year goal, two months ahead of schedule. I was out of debt and on my way to even greater success. This was by no means easy but anything is possible if you want it bad enough and are willing to put in the time and effort required to achieve it.

One of the big things I have learnt on my journey to success is that positivity is the catalyst for success. It drives all the desire, passion and determination that is inside of you. I'm a firm believer that if you truly believe in yourself, no one will ever be able to break you. This mindset paves the way forward and opens so many new doors and opportunities.

I wake up every single morning knowing today will be better than yesterday. I truly believe you become what you think about. Everything I have achieved now has come from my attitude and surrounding myself with positive, can-do people.

The first thing I do every single morning is listen to an inspiring audio. Nothing beats the sound of inspiring words in the mornings and that is how my day continues and it flows right through my family, to my staff and to my customers. How happy are you when you wake up to the sound of your own opportunity clock, instead of your alarm clock? The morning is the best time to seize that opportunity and look at things from a different perspective. The thoughts behind the words you speak create your attitude.

Understanding your life balance is also another key element to being successful and this is something I truly learnt the hard way. I used to believe that the harder and longer I worked, the more successful I would become. How wrong could I be? It was not until I experienced my first breakdown that this really hit home and I was in a state of shock. I didn't know what was going on. My mind was telling me to pull myself together, yet my body just could not go on anymore and it shut down on me. I now make sure I have at least three holidays per year with my family so that my body gets the rest it needs. I also make sure that whenever I want to do something that I enjoy, I make time for it.

We all know that eating healthy and getting plenty of exercise is crucial. A healthy body and a healthy mind equals a healthy life. Being healthy and having a can-do attitude gives you the opportunity to be the most remarkable person that you can be. It releases the greatness inside of you. The minute you understand this and implement it, your life changes for the better, so open your eyes and see how contagious a positive attitude can be. It was a game changer for me, so I hope you can embrace it too and it helps you realise your own dreams.

Contact:

gary@watfordbathroomsandkitchens.co.uk

ELEMENT TEN: HELP!: HOW THE ENTREPRENEURS CIRCLE CAN HELP YOU ON YOUR JOURNEY

Would you like to take your entrepreneurial journey to the 'accountability' level and beyond? You've probably had more than a glimpse of the type of coaching we give our members by the quality of the information in this book, and we run over 100 different courses at our National Support Centre in Birmingham and in the South of England, plus monthly regional events and have different levels of membership to match all types of business types. If you want to grow your own business and make a positive impact on more of your customer's lives, then please visit: www.EntrepreneursCircle.org to find out more.

My own website has resources available on it and you can sign up to my 'Rethink' emails:

www.RethinkingBusiness.biz

You can also email me at

Damian@RethinkingBusiness.biz

And please feel free to join the Facebook group:

www.facebook.com/entrepreneursuccessformula

RESOURCES AND LINKS

Entrepreneurs Circle: entrepreneurscircle.org

Hubspot: hubspot.com

Social Media Examiner: socialmediaexaminer.com

Entrepreneur on Fire: eofire.com

Bulletproof Radio: bulletproofexec.com

Tim Ferris Podcast:

fourhourworkweek.com/podcast

Infusionsoft: go.infusionsoft.com

MailChimp: mailchimp.com

Aweber: aweber.com

Three Principles Movies:

threeprinciplesmovies.com

OneFocus App: onefocusapp.com

Dropbox.com

Books:
Botty's Rules by Nigel Botterill

Build your Business in 90 Minutes a Day by Martin Gladdish and Nigel Botterill

Do Nothing! Stop Looking, Start Living by Damian Mark Smyth

Will it Make the Boat go Faster by Ben Hunt-Davis

The E-Myth Revisited by Michael E. Gerber

Start with Why by Simon Sinek

Think and Grow Rich by Napoleon Hill

The Compound Effect by Darren Hardy

Life in Half a Second by Matthew Michalewicz

Clarity by Jamie Smart

The Entrepreneur Revolution by Daniel Priestley

Oversubscribed by Daniel Priestley

Miracle Morning by Hal Elrod

The Lean Startup by Eric Ries

The Millionaire Fastlane by M. J. DeMarco

80/20 Sales and Marketing by Perry Marshall

Influence by Robert B. Cialdini

Rework by David Heinemeier Hansson and Jason Fried

Start Your Business in 7 Days by James Caan

Entrepreneur Success Formula

ONE FINAL THOUGHT

"Until one is committed, there is hesitancy, the chance to draw back... Concerning all acts of initiative (and creation) there is one elementary truth that ignorance of which kills countless ideas and splendid plans: that the moment one definitely commits oneself, then Providence moves too.

All sorts of things occur to help one that would never otherwise have occurred.

A whole stream of events issues from the decision, raising in one's favor all manner of unforeseen incidents and meetings and material assistance, which no man could have dreamed would have come his way.

Whatever you can do, or dream you can do, begin it.

Boldness has genius, power, and magic in it. Begin it now."

- Johann Wolfgang von Goethe

NOTES

NOTES

The only surefire way to accurately
predict the future is to create it.
So get started... NOW!

We hope you've found this book useful,
so please spread the word using the
hashtag #ECWorks on social media and
kindly post a review on Amazon.

Thank you.

Damian Smyth

$-150 \times 60.$

$1500 \times$
$\quad 12$
6
$\overline{18000}$

$.720$
$^2\times 12$
$\overline{14440}$
7200
1480
$\overline{8680}$

3
9000
8680
$\overline{17680}$

15000